Horn of Africa

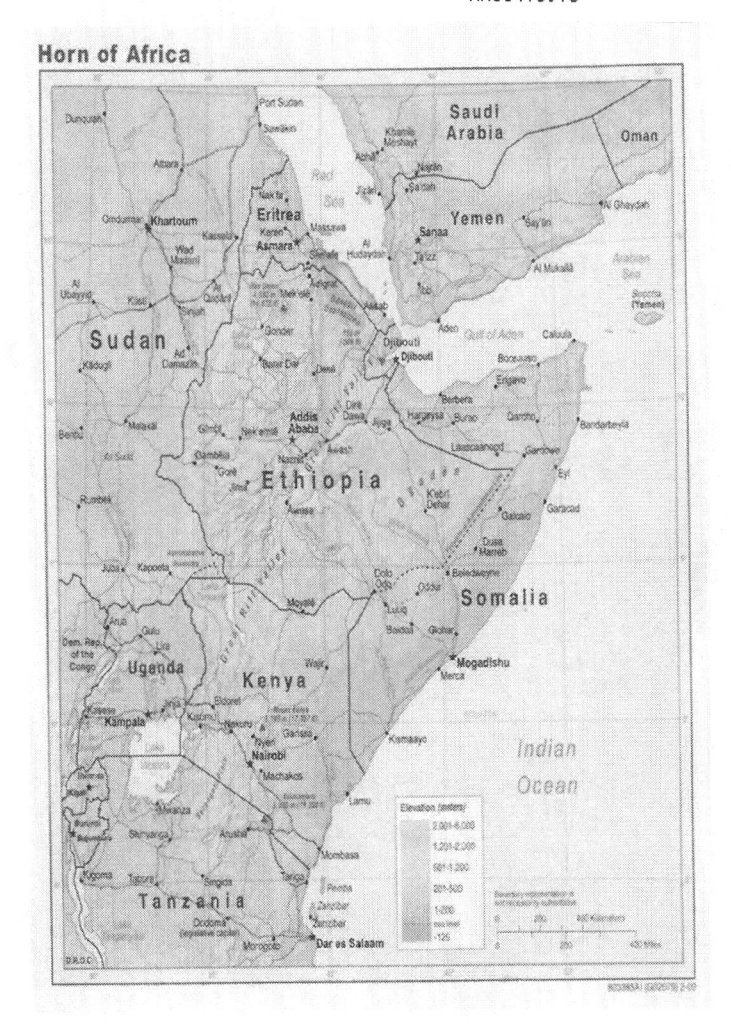

An Unexpected Journey

Somalia 1992-1994

By

Anthony Dillett

Copyright © Anthony Dillett 2014

ISBN 978-1500321598

An Unexpected Journey – Somalia 1992-1993 is an original work written and copyrighted by Anthony A Dillett

All rights reserved. No part of this publication may be reproduced, stored in a retrieval system, or transmitted in any form or by any means electronic, mechanical, photocopying, recording or otherwise without the prior written permission of the copyright holder.

LOC Registration TX 7-901-345 Anthony A Dillett

Reviews

A compelling story full of suspense and mystery, and almost reads like fiction. It is well written, and keeps the reader spell bound with all that is happening in these countries. Danger seems to be everywhere, with people constantly running for their lives. An excellent account and extremely well written.

Joy Abbas, Author, Fan Story

Unbelievably difficult story to tell... yet it's told in a straight-forward way. It's told with detail, emotion and a real intent to impart the truth.

Lois Loanna, Author

Powerful and descriptive words that allow the reader to step into a political and social hornet's nest. It kept my interest from beginning to end. Well done.

Gracie Ann, Author

You (Anthony Dillett) are one fine writer. This work is outstanding in so many ways. Your writer's "voice" is comfortable to listen to and your imagery is superb. Like: "In the Western world, there are fences or hedges to mark boundaries. However, in Mogadishu there are 12-foot walls that separate properties. The roofs of the buildings are flat and are generally used by the family for recreation in the cool of the evening..."

Bob Mastery, Author

This story is one of the best stories I had read the past few months. It was very real, active, moving and penetrating. From beginning to end, I marveled at the way it was written. A narrative that strikes the senses. I could see clearly the events... the dangers and the writer's experiences.

Dom G. Robles, Engineer

This book is about personal suffering and the human tragedy that evolved into the failed State of Somalia in the Horn of Africa. It is unlike the journalism of the book "Blackhawk Down" and the sensationalism of the spin-off motion picture of the same name.

"An Unexpected Journey" is truly an up-close and personal experience of the author who danced with the Devil and played Russian roulette with death. I cannot say that I enjoyed this book. "Enjoyed" would not be the appropriate word to describe what I felt. Yet, I could not put it down .It gripped me. It handcuffed me to my chair. I was hooked and I was captivated.

It is unlike any other book I have read before. As a childhood friend of the author with a close friendship that has lasted more than sixty years but with a brief hiatus, I was not aware of his horrendous experience, working as an international civil servant with the United Nations. Although both he and his wife Raquel shared snippets, this is like the book of Revelations - a revelation to me. It is also, perhaps, about AD's humility and the strength of his character that he chooses, initially, not to share his journey to hell and back when we visited with each other after his horrendous experience.

This book is powerful. The author is a man of substance who stands "skyscraper" tall. I am diminished by the magnitude of AD's journey – a journey that did not negatively affect his gentleness, his humanity or his spirit. It is a must-read to understand the mess that is Somalia. The reader will learn of the Clinton Administration's ill-informed and ill-advised political decisions that influenced the problems that persist, even today, in this failed State of Somalia.

An Unexpected Journey: Somalia 1992-1993 is well written, well researched, intimate and compelling.

I give it five stars.

Norris Hall
Journalist

Contents

Introduction xi

Prologue - How did I get here? xiv

1. New Experiences 1

2. Restore Hope 25

3. A Different Place 33

4. The Unprotected 47

5. Inshallah (God Willing) 56

6. The Vulnerable 69

7. In the Wrong Place 83

8. U.S. Rangers Assault U.N. Employees 92

9. Post-Traumatic Stress 117

10. A Killer Disease 129

11. The Struggle to Leave Nairobi 139

12. Diagnosis and Prognosis 150

13. The Operation 167

14. The Cure 182

15. Revelation 197

Epilogue: The Man at the Gate 206

About the Author 208

Dedication

I dedicate this book to my wife, Raquel, whose love, loyalty and steadfastness sustained me in good times and bad. It is also dedicated to my children Alex, Paul, Jennifer and Melanie who spurred me on to write the story of my sojourn in Somalia; particularly to Melanie and her original poem, "God's Will". She wrote it in the Waiting Room at Lenox Hill Hospital as my family waited for news on the operation that would determine whether I lived or died. Writing the Somalia story was also important for my grandchildren Le Shaun, Damian, AJ, Shayla, Adrian, Nathaniel and Mikailah, and my great-grandson Josiah. I wanted them to have a glimpse into the difficulties people face in other places, and how fortunate they are to live in this country, even with the shortcomings of its people.

Dr. Kevin Cahill was instrumental in reminding my wife of the power of prayer when he told her that my chance of surviving the illness, that had taken hold of me, was in God's hands. If you believe in God, he had told my wife, you must get down on your hands and knees and ask God to spare your husband's life. The combined skills of my medical team, Dr. Cahill had said, cannot save his life

I would be remiss if I did not mention my brother KC. He gave me a laptop when mine went on the blink with the comment that a writer cannot write without writing tools. I also owe a debt of gratitude to two childhood friends, John Locke and Wayne Rhys. Our many conversations, during the time it took me to finish this book, invariable ended with: "How's the book coming?"

Last but not least are the many relatives and friends who prayed me through those very difficult times when my life hung in a balance. They epitomized the faith of the men who knew that their crippled friend would be healed if they brought his plight to Jesus' attention:

"Seeing their faith, He said, "Friend, your sins are forgiven you".
Luke 5:20 (NASB)

Introduction

The United States intervention in Somalia in 1992, on humanitarian grounds, is very relevant today, over twenty years later, as we witness the events unfolding in Iraq, Syria and The Yemen. The Kurds, a people without a homeland, is also central to the problem that seems insolvable at this time. In the current situation the U.S. involvement is not altogether altruistic. There are policies in place to protect the country from the threat posed by those who, given the chance, would destroy our way of life. This does not, of course, take away from a genuine desire to render humanitarian assistance to those in need.

The news of the U. S. and other countries' involvement in trying to alleviate the suffering of millions of people, mentions military intervention, coalition forces and destroying the perceived threat to peace. However, the general public is unaware of attempts being made to understand the people they have, ostensibly, been sworn to assist. If anything, the Somali debacle should have taught the U.S. that military might and bureaucratic arrogance cannot replace a genuine interest in what makes other people tick. In other words every attempt should be made to see people as we see ourselves, and not as those poor people who need help. Perhaps the Somali story, as seen through the eyes of a lowly civil servant, will help to make people, all over the world, view each other with compassion and respect.

The suggestion may be regarded as simplistic from an extremely complicated political, historical and cultural viewpoint. Politicians, bureaucrats and the military have been involved in the process for decades with little or no success; so what do we have to lose in trying another approach.

* * *

Tony Dillett is on a humanitarian mission with the United Nations Development Programme (UNDP) in Somalia in 1992-1993. It is an extremely dangerous assignment. The civil war that ended in January 1991, left a vacuum in which anarchy reigned supreme. The population is being decimated by a famine that would eventually claim the lives of some 350,000 Somalis.

The U.N. Security Council establishes the United Nations Office in Somalia (UNOSOM) in April 1992. Pakistani Peacekeepers form part of UNOSOM's mandate and try to stem the violence, but are unable to do so.

Before leaving office, President George H W Bush intervenes in Somalia on humanitarian grounds. The first contingent of U.S. forces, that would eventually total 25,000, arrives in Somalia January 9, 1993 and the security situation improves. However, after his inauguration in January 1993, President Bill Clinton announces a reduction in the number of soldiers to 1,200 by May 1993. The planned reduction emboldens the warring factions to resume attacks on each other and U.S forces.

On June 5, 1993 twenty-four Pakistani Peacekeepers are killed by General Mohamed Farrah Aidid's militia. U.S. Rangers are deployed to capture Aidid. On August 30, 1993, Tony's residence is mistakenly attacked by the Rangers, he is assaulted and subsequently suffers from PTSD. He is in Mogadishu during the "Black Hawk

Down" incident. He learns afterwards that armored vehicles and Bradley tanks, requested by Officers commanding the troops, were not approved by the bureaucrats in Washington, placing the troops at risk.

Tony is in Nairobi in mid-November 1993, where he becomes ill and is diagnosed with a virulent strain of typhoid fever. Providentially his wife, Raquel, is with him one night as he goes into shock and would have died but for her decisive action. Raquel takes Tony to New York where he is also diagnosed with an infected abdominal aortic aneurysm. Tony's doctor tells Raquel that she should pray for divine intervention because the combined medical skills at Lenox Hill Hospital cannot save his life...

Prologue

How Did I Get Here?

Pain insists upon being attended to. God whispers to us in our pleasures, speaks in our consciences, but shouts in our pains. It is his megaphone to rouse a deaf world."
C.S. Lewis

The pain was excruciating, ripping through my body and brought tears to my eyes. I felt the pain just below my rib cage in a spot the doctor had told us, my wife and me, would signal the end of my life. I thought I was dying, lying on my bed, in a fetal position that somehow seemed to take the edge off the pain. According to the doctor that type of discomfort meant the graft, that had replaced a section of my abdominal aorta just a few months before, had ruptured and there was nothing anyone could do to save my life. I would die from excessive bleeding even if I were on the Operating Table.

The doctor's voice was devoid of any emotions, matter of fact, without concern for the effect such a possibility held for us. It was not that he did not feel the anxiety caused by the death sentence he had passed on me shortly after the operation. The doctor was tired, physically and mentally, after nine hours in the Operating Room. True that was three days before the warning of impending disaster, but he was languishing in the aftermath of the most difficult and yes, most satisfying results of any operation he had undertaken up to that point in his professional career. The graft was the first successful outcome to repair a typhoid damaged aorta, according to the medical associations in the United States and Europe. The doctor's accomplishments were fleeting thoughts that, while important, were irrelevant at that point in my life as I waited, with some trepidation, to take my last breath.

I knew that my time had come and, as I imagined that my life was slipping away, thoughts of how I got to where I was kept cropping up in my mind. Something was forcing me to go back and look at the circumstances leading up to the doctor's prediction, and my waiting for the end as my life ebbed away. How did I get here? That, it seemed, was a necessary question that I had to answer. So I allowed my thoughts to drift to Somalia, the place where my ordeal began.

1

New Experiences

"Do you know the difference between education and experience?
Education is when you read the fine print;
Experience is what you get when you don't"
Pete Seeger

I arrived in Mogadishu, Somalia early in November 1992 to take up the assignment as Operations Manager with the United Nations Development Programme (UNDP). The airport was bustling with activity as Somali men, armed with all types of weapons—M16s, Kalashnikov, rocket launchers, automatic pistols and hand grenades casually moved about, some in agitated conversation. I could not understand a word they were saying, but gleaned that there was some measure of discontent among them. I had never been close to so many weapons and, for a moment as I stood there taking in the scene, I wondered if I were on a movie set and expected to hear "CUT" at any minute.

However, the director's command never came. At the same time I realized that I was not on a movie set, I was jerked out of my reverie by a booming sound in the distance that could only have emanated from the discharge of heavy artillery. This was really happening; the scenes I had seen on television and the chaos I had read about were facts. I thought about what I had gotten myself into with an overwhelming sense of dread. I regretted, after only half an hour in the country, that I had not read the fine print in the report on Somalia. I wanted desperately to turn the clock back to the day when I was offered and accepted the post in Somalia, but turning the clock back was not an option.

It was at that point that I had an epiphany, nothing divine, but rather a sudden clear understanding of what lay ahead. Before agreeing to the assignment in Somalia, I had been employed by UNDP for some twenty years and had worked in New York, a number of countries in the Caribbean and Africa. My wife Raquel and daughters Jennifer and Melanie had accompanied me on those assignments, even in difficult places like Angola and Sierra Leone. The only place that had raised some level of concern for my wife was Angola in the early 1980s. The country was in the throes of a civil war with parts of its southern territory under South African control. Somalia, for my wife, was reminiscent of Angola and, as soon as I told her of the assignment, she had a premonition of disaster and shared her feelings with me. Her warning, and what I had observed as soon as I stepped off the airplane, sent shivers down my spine.

The driver of the vehicle UNDP had sent to pick me up from the airport was an amicable young man named Hassan. He drove me through a section of the city that had not been destroyed in the civil war. However, time and neglect had left their mark on almost all the structures I saw. A number of buildings were hidden from view by walls at least 12 feet high. If the condition of the walls replicated what lay behind, extensive work would be required to restore the buildings to their former glory or, at least, make them less of an eye sore.

In the Western world, there are fences or hedges to mark boundaries. However, in Mogadishu there are 12-foot walls that separate properties. The roofs of the buildings are flat and are used by the family for recreation in the cool of the evening. The beauty of the Indian Ocean, with its gently rippling white-capped waves and endless blue stretching into the distance, can be seen from most rooftops.

As we approached an area of the city known as Kilometer 5, I observed a fork in the road. The driver told me that the right fork led to the United Nations Operation in Somalia (UNOSOM) and the left to the UNDP office. Those roads soon became the ones most traveled by me during my stay in Mogadishu. The one that caused me anxiety, dread actually, was the road to UNOSOM. About half a mile from the junction where the road forked, was the largest refugee camp in Mogadishu. I came to dislike going down that road because of my experiences while visiting the camp for ongoing needs assessments, supervising food deliveries and camp security.

After each visit, the smell of the camp lingered with me for hours and sometimes for days because of the odor of unwashed bodies, feces and urine. There were makeshift toilets in the camp, and they would have been able to contain excrement and urine provided they were used as intended. However, that was not always the case. Some people stooped, relieved themselves whenever the need arose and moved on. Such actions resulted in exacerbating the unhealthy conditions of the camp. The thing that bothered me the most, however, was the plight of the children. As things stood, their future was bleak forever scrounging around to stay alive amid the chaos with no end in sight. Those thoughts, experiences and feelings, would manifest themselves later. In the meantime, my mind was occupied with the road we were traveling on and the people we passed on our way.

The driver took me straight to a two-story building, about ten miles from the Airport that served as the offices of UNDP and the World Food Programme (WFP). The gate to the compound opened, and I had my second experience that had the potential for violence. Blocking our path was a jeep with a sub-machine gun mounted just behind the driver. I knew that type of vehicle was called a "Technical" from what I had seen on television. I learned later that the word originated with Relief workers. They did not want to admit to their superiors in Europe that they had to pay for protection, so they listed the service provided as "Technical Assistance."

A youth, of no more than fifteen years, sat behind the sub-machine gun and pointed it directly at us. The blast from the gun was, in my mind, as inevitable as my next breath. My heart raced, but did not escape from my mouth because my throat had constricted to such an extent that I was, at the same time, gasping for breath. As my heart raced, and my throat constricted, I had a tremendous need to go to the toilet. But I had to be absolutely still to keep my heart in check, my throat from completely closing up, and the mechanism in my body from releasing the unmentionables.

The youth held up a hand just like a traffic cop and disdainfully gestured to my driver to move aside. That was my first experience in which someone pointed a weapon in my general direction, not at me personally. The fact that it was not personal had zero calming effect on me. Experience taught many people in Somalia not to argue with a Technical, so my driver moved aside, although it would have been easier if the Technical had waited for us to pass.

That was my experience the first day in Somalia. The incident was apparently commonplace since no one, except me, paid any attention to it, or thought it significant enough to discuss. The UNDP Representative, Peter Schuman, was on the second floor balcony, and had witnessed the incident, but did not comment except to say in a loud voice, "Welcome to Somalia!" It seemed to me that he was both amused and bemused by the obvious fear that had gripped me.

The incident passed, and everything inside me returned to normal. The crisis of the toilet was forgotten. I wondered if the need were a figment of my imagination, and if I had actually felt such fear. Perhaps my body had acted unreasonably after taking its lead from my brain. It had been unable to process all that had happened since my arrival in Somalia. It was reasonable, therefore, that the reaction would be exaggerated and cause the symptoms of anxiety. I concluded that my brain was over stimulated, and had given off the wrong signals. I told myself that I would be better able to cope with similar situations in the future. Or would I?

The building was dilapidated, and I made a mental note that a face-lift was in order. Even the staff I met needed a boost of some kind to lift their spirits. Initially, I could not figure out why everyone seemed preoccupied. They acted as if something was hanging over their collective heads that spelled imminent disaster. I should have taken my cue from my experience at the airport, but somehow the incident had receded in the past as if it had not occurred. And then I remembered as a thunderous boom was heard that shook the very foundations of our building. It rattled the windows, and caused the desks and chairs to shimmy a few inches as if we were experiencing an earthquake.

"Is it nearer, or is that a figment of my imagination?" Peter Schuman asked no one in particular.

"No," Larry DuBois, the Deputy Representative, replied. "It seems as if they are using bigger canons today."

The banter was exchanged in a matter of fact way as one would expect in a regular conversation. However, there was an undertone, a hint of fear that had become an integral part of everyday life in Mogadishu. The bombardment continued for several minutes, and then ceased just as abruptly as it had begun.

It occurred to me that not one person had moved during the brief exchange of artillery. No one said anything, except for the brief exchange between Peter and Larry. Everyone had been preoccupied with their own thoughts—their personal fears, not knowing where the shells had landed; perhaps in one of their neighborhoods? Then the shelling stopped, and everyone resumed their activities as if there had not been a pause in what they had been doing. The transition, from being frozen in silence and the resumption of what was going on before, was seamless.

Peter ushered me into a sparsely furnished office overlooking the guardhouse and the street used to access the main road. He sat down and indicated that I should sit behind the desk that was adorned with a telephone, nothing else. A young man, who later identified himself only as Abdi, one of the office messengers, came into the room and asked Peter and me if we wanted some tea. Peter said yes, for both of us, but without milk. The "without milk" was said with some emphasis. I said nothing, but the quizzical look on my face prompted Peter to explain, without my asking, why he said no milk.

"I am assuming that you have not had camel's milk before," he said. "Somalis are partial to tea with milk, and the only milk that is usually available is unpasteurized camel's milk. I need not elaborate on that I am sure."

"Thanks for the warning," was my reply. "If I had known you were short of creamer, I would have brought some from Nairobi. Actually, I drink tea with or without milk."

"We usually have an ample supply," Peter said, "but we ran out a few days ago. I was so preoccupied with other matters that it slipped my mind to replenish our stock. Additionally, the tea is aromatic and brewed with some spices making milk quite unnecessary."

A few minutes later Abdi returned with a huge pot of tea and three cups. Soon after that Larry joined us and, after asking about my journey, and my initial impressions of Mogadishu, both Peter and Larry took turns briefing me on the situation in Somalia, and general operational procedures. The session started with a statement that the United Nations (U.N.) system, in Somalia, was being held hostage by the most powerful clans in the country. I had read something on the subject in the country report for Somalia, but said nothing waiting for them to elaborate, which they did without embellishments, just plain facts.

Mogadishu, and most of the country, are unlike any place in the civilized world. Law and order, that are taken for granted in most places, were replaced with vigilante justice. The standing army was disbanded in the early days of the civil war, and the soldiers were incorporated into the various militias that were formed along clan lines. Some became members of marauding groups that roamed the country robbing, confiscating property and committing all types of atrocities. The same held true for the national police force. The chaos that ensued made the entire country unsafe without armed security to protect life and property. Somalis lived in clan based communities that provided some measure of security. However, everyone lived in fear, and had to depend on family to assist in keeping them safe within their neighborhoods. But that type of protection did not guarantee safety and, as a result, some people suffered. The dangers of living in that situation were multiplied tenfold when people had to leave their communities for whatever reason. Many lost their property to gangs or worse, were killed in the streets, and their bodies discarded like so much trash.

The United Nations and humanitarian organizations would have been in the same predicament, but for the practice of employing armed guards to protect offices and residences, and "Technicals" for travel anywhere in the country. Each organization leased buildings for offices and residences next to each other, or were separated by no more than about 100 feet. As a group, the organizations were no more than twenty miles from the airport. A good arrangement, for security reasons, in case an evacuation of the city became necessary. The disadvantage was that Mogadishu was a sprawling city of some 640 square miles, with about 300 square miles falling within the southern part of the city.

The offices and residences were scattered within that part of the city, and would prove to be a problem later. Just as significant was the fact that south Mogadishu was Aidid's territory. He was the most belligerent warlord, and opposed the United Nations intervention in Somalia any time he could. Aidid's distrust and animosity towards the United Nations were personal. He had a long-standing grudge against the United Nations Secretary General, Boutros Boutros-Ghali; who was a close ally of the deposed Somali dictator, Siad Barre.

In addition to having some control over the buildings that were rented by the International Community, every driver, clerk, guard and translator who was hired was somehow tied to Aidid. That meant that the Community involuntarily contributed to Aidid's war chest, which in turn fueled the conflict. The Community hoped that having to deal, commercially, with Aidid's minions was a short term disadvantage. The long-term goal to eliminate starvation, and assist in the reconciliation process were the important objectives. However, there were those skeptics who predicted anything but a satisfactory outcome in the long run.

At that point in the discussion, Larry chimed in and gave a fairly comprehensive, but succinct history of the process that led to Somalia being declared a failed state.

In 1990, the U.N. and humanitarian agencies evacuated their staff from Somalia to Nairobi, Kenya, during the height of the civil war. Temporary offices had been set up in Nairobi to keep track of what was happening in Somalia. From their bases in Nairobi, numerous missions went into Mogadishu, and other cities to monitor the conditions in the country; discuss arrangements for peace talks with clan leaders, and make assessments of what could be done to alleviate the suffering of the Somalis. Food and medical supplies were also brought into the country, but were pilfered by gangs operating in consort with the major clan leaders.

After the downfall of the dictator, Siad Barre, in January 1991 there was a power struggle between two factions, one led by the Interim President Ali Mahdi Mohamed and the other by General Mohammad Farrah Aidid. Those factions were, in fact, allies in the fight to depose Siad Barre. The discord between them was further complicated by the fact that they were members of related sub-clans, the Abgal and Habar Gidir. That meant they were members of the same family—cousins, in other words, but the pursuit of power negated any clan relationship.

Ali Mahdi was a businessman and politician. He had used his resources and considerable influence in the war to depose Siad Barre. Aidid was the soldier/politician who was personally involved on the battle fronts to free Somalia of the dictator. The agreement between these two leaders was that Aidid would be appointed President of the country once hostilities ceased. However, while Aidid was hundreds of miles from Mogadishu in a mop-up operation to ensure the total destruction of Siad Barre's army, Ali Mahdi convened a meeting of the clans that were allied to him, and on their authority declared himself President of the Republic of Somalia. When news of the betrayal reached Aidid, he returned to Mogadishu with his militia and attacked Ali Mahdi and his allies.

By November 1991, the most intensive fighting was going on in Mogadishu between the two factions causing hundreds of thousands of Somalis to flee from their homes. A section of the once beautiful city was destroyed in the bombardment as opposing forces vied for control of the city. The deteriorating conditions did not go unnoticed by the U.N. and other International Organizations as images of starving people, mostly women and children, were seen on television and reported on in newspapers. The violence was exacerbated by a drought and ensuing famine that would claim the lives of over 350,000 Somalis. Nearly 1,000,000 Somalis became refugees in Kenya and Ethiopia.

Individual countries, it appeared, were inattentive and did not care sufficiently about the plight of the Somali people. Most of them, including the United States, France, Russia, England, Japan and The Netherlands paid little, if any, attention to the carnage. European countries were busily involved in the war, in Bosnia, while the United States was engaged with its own domestic affairs after declaring victory in Operation Desert Storm in February 1991. The country was also saddled with a recession and high unemployment that persisted for the rest of the year. Even African countries took a hands-off approach except for Ethiopia and Kenya that were impacted directly by the refugee problem.

However, while those countries were engrossed with their political and economic limitations, they were involved in Somalia jointly through the U.N. Security Council. Agencies such as the International Committee of the Red Cross also had boots on the ground in Somalia, even under the most difficult and dangerous situations.

An incident to illustrate the extremely dangerous working conditions in Somalia formed a part of the brief. In January 1992, a UNICEF doctor was killed in Bosasso, a city some 900 miles north of Mogadishu. She was sent there to evaluate the situation on the ground. While dining one evening with a friend, she was gunned down by masked men. The assassins were never found, but some people believed that they belonged to a group of fundamentalists from outside the country. They had taken control of the city and wanted to send a message that foreign intervention would not be tolerated.

The United Nations brokered a cease-fire among the warring factions in March 1992. The following month, April 1992, the U.N. Security Council approved the establishment of the United Nations Operation in Somalia (UNOSOM) headed by Special Representative Mohammed Sahnoun from Algeria. UNOSOM's mandate included monitoring the ceasefire in Mogadishu, and escorting convoys delivering humanitarian supplies to distribution centers in the city. The mission's mandate was later expanded, enabling it to protect humanitarian convoys and distribution centers throughout the country. The total strength of UNOSOM was to be some 4,200 personnel, including 500 unarmed military observers from Pakistan, headed by Brig. Gen Imtiaz Shaheen.

UNOSOM's efforts were hampered, from the start, by clan violence. The military observers and security personnel were prevented from carrying out their duties because heavily armed militias, allied to Aidid, looted food and medical supplies. They also attacked incoming and docked ships, and cargo planes at the airport, that carried humanitarian aid for Somalia. The military observers and security personnel were powerless to stop the looting and help with food delivery. They too faced violence and could not respond because of their limited mandate. Additionally, they did not have the firepower or the capability to resist when they were threatened or attacked.

Shortly after UNOSOM established its presence in Somalia in April 1992 UNDP, the United Nations Children's Emergency Fund (UNICEF), the Food and Agricultural Organization (FAO) and The

World Food Programme (WFP) returned to Somalia. However, their activities were also hampered by lawlessness and continued clan violence. In spite of the dangers, and the lack of adequate security, UNDP and other humanitarian agencies tried to provide a number of services to Somalia while laying the groundwork for a fully functioning government after hostilities ceased.

One of the main UNDP projects was management of the Port of Mogadishu. It was next to impossible to control activities in the Port to offload, store and deliver food and medical supplies to the refugee camps and feeding centers. The constant high alert to arrange protection to transport supplies consumed a great deal of time. Quite often most of the food and supplies were hijacked between the Port and delivery sites. The conditions produced stress, even among the heartiest aid workers. Nevertheless, the weekly effort to make deliveries continued with varying degrees of success.

Another important UNDP project involved Mogadishu's water supply. The water-supply system had suffered from neglect, with the warring factions fighting over its control, which carried with it both political and military power. Even as they struggled over hegemony, the factions were confronted with the considerable cost of keeping the city adequately supplied with water. That was where UNDP's role in providing technical support was utilized to revamp the water supply system for Mogadishu.

There were sufficient ground water reserves, but it was a challenge to get the water to ground level and into homes without financial and, just as necessary, expert professional inputs. Highly qualified engineers and hydrologists were employed by UNDP to ensure the system worked efficiently and guarantee that water quality was maintained. Mogadishu is on the shores of the Indian Ocean, and care had to be taken to safeguard that fresh water from the wells was not contaminated by salt water from the sea. Within a month of taking over the supply system, the wells were producing more than sufficient water for the entire city.

UNDP also executed a sanitation project. Imagine years of garbage piled up on every street in the city, not being collected and without a garbage dump. The smell of rotting garbage permeated the city, and beyond its borders. As can be imagined, the situation added to the unhealthy conditions in the city. As my colleagues spoke, I felt a sense of pride to be involved in UNDP's humanitarian efforts in Somalia. They were certainly not without fault, but the greatest seemed to be having leaders who cared nothing about their welfare; leaders whose focus were on acquiring power no matter who suffered, who starved or how many people died.

The conversation then turned to the people, and their struggles to regain a semblance of their past independence, and their proud standing in the world. In a way, some in the International Community were sympathetic to their plight, and turned a blind eye to the obvious extortion being perpetrated by unscrupulous landlords and security providers. The Community was cognizant of the fact that they were powerless to do anything about the situation—pay for protection or suffer the consequences.

There were no industries, except for the scattered herds of goats and camels that roamed the countryside to the north of Mogadishu. However, only a very small sector of the population benefitted from that source of income.

There was an export market to the Middle East for livestock, but all that had little, if any, effect on the economy of the country. The agricultural industry in the south was decimated by the civil war and drought. Since no government existed, what little revenue that could have been derived from exporting livestock and agricultural products was not being collected.

Peter felt that it was necessary for me to get some information on the people I was in Somalia to assist. He sent for a UNDP consultant on Somali affairs, who just happened to be in the office when I arrived. I was introduced to John Drysdale, an Englishman, who had lived in the country, among various clans for over forty years. He was the commanding officer for a platoon of Somalis during World War II, became fascinated with his subordinates and, after the war, took up residence in Mogadishu.

John was fluent in Somali, and had gained the respect of the leading clan elders, political and military leaders in the country. He remained in Somalia during the worst days of the civil war, trying to broker peace agreements among the factions with little or no success. His obvious love of the country and Somalis endeared him to people in general and specifically to the leading figures in the country.

My session with John did not take long. He began his brief by saying that there were two versions of the origins of the Somali people. One held that the clans and sub-clans descended from two brothers Samaale and Sab. Samaale and his wife are the ancestors of the major clans Dir, Isaaq, Hawiye and Daarood and that Sab fathered the Digil and Rahanweyn clans. The Samaale group of clans is primarily nomadic with herds of camels and goats. They occupy most of northern and central Somalia, parts of Ethiopia, Kenya and Djibouti. Sab clans inhabit the southern region of Somalia and are engaged in farming and herding.

The second theory posits that Somalis descend from the lineage of the Prophet Mohammad. However, that version has been discounted by scholars because of archaeological, linguistic and cultural evidence that points to Cush, in the Highlands of Ethiopia, as the ancestral home of Samaale and Sab. John believed that the culture of the Somalis, in which blood relationships took precedence over everything else, was the primary reason for the deplorable situation in the country.

He quoted two Somali proverbs that contained a wealth of information about the people, and explained a cultural perspective that is alien to people in the West. The first proverb dealt with Somali relationships within the clan and sub-clan structures and their view of outsiders.

"A man and his brother against the cousin; a man and his cousin against the stranger."

The second proverb spoke to how warm the embrace would be when Somalis inquired one of the other:

"Somalis do not ask each other **where** they are from but rather **whom** they are from."

The important point to note, John said, was that everything in Somalia started with the clan or family. Every man, woman and child's alliance was vested in the clan. They were members of a particular clan or sub-clan first and foremost followed by the national designation of being Somali. They were a complicated people, and unless the UN and other agencies realized they were not dealing with a ragtag group of ignorant nomads; good intentions would turn into a disaster. John felt deeply for these people and expressed his thoughts to anyone who would listen. He believed he was Somali in another life, which would explain his empathy for, and feeling of, belonging to Somalia.

My role as Operations Manager was fairly easy in terms of complexity. I was the designated officer for certifying expenditure of some $400,000 per month to fund UNDP projects in Mogadishu and other parts of the country; negotiating leases for offices and living quarters; and managing the activities of fifteen local and two international staff. The duties that consumed most of my time during the day, and sometimes late in the night, was the security of staff in an unsafe environment. It entailed handling twenty-four guards and ensuring that a viable security plan, showing evacuation routes, was always up-to-date. I also oversaw the activities of the Medical Clinic that played an indispensable role in keeping staff healthy.

Logistically, my job was a nightmare. It was difficult to find appropriate and fairly safe accommodation. Supplying food and ensuring that it was prepared in a healthy environment was next to impossible. We had to make sure that the cooks and service staff adhered to the health rules that had been set in place. Medical examinations were performed regularly, but since testing blood, stool and urine were primitive at best, we had to depend on divine intervention to keep us fairly healthy.

My first visit to the kitchen, on my second day in Mogadishu, sent shivers down my spine. Flies were everywhere feasting undisturbed on meat, bread, fruit or whatever was left uncovered. A perfunctory inspection of the kitchen revealed broken screens for doors and windows, and counters that were covered with congealed blood that, obviously, had not been cleaned for only God knew how long. I did not dare to conduct any further inspection because I was afraid of what I might find.

I immediately ordered that all the food, cooked and uncooked, were disposed of, and I directed an aide to ensure that my instructions were carried out. I suspected that all that food found its way in some homes or a refugee camp. In reality, I felt that was better than destroying food in a place where so many people were starving. I was conflicted in allowing food that I knew to be unhealthy, to leave the premises, but I did not ask where it went. Next I sent for a carpenter and had the screens on the doors and windows repaired. The exterminator came, and took care of rodents that had, as I had suspected, taken up residence in the kitchen. Cleaning the counters was also accomplished. The cook was given strict instructions. No food was to be left uncovered or prepared outside the confines of the kitchen. For about a week, breakfast, lunch and dinner consisted of fruit, canned meats, crackers, coffee, tea and honey.

The cook was a man, and since I did not trust him to follow the new standards, I hired a woman to supervise him, those who worked with him and those who kept our residence clean. I also talked to the cook and told him, in no uncertain terms, that I was not satisfied with how things were under his supervision. I did not want to fire him because I was sure his family was dependent on him. However, I informed him that if I found any infraction of the rules, I would have no choice but to let him go. He was grateful for the consideration shown to him. He did well and adhered to the rules that were established. He remained in our employment until the office was relocated, once more, to Nairobi in June 1993.

Days passed without any significant incident, except for the constant sound of weapons being discharged, sometimes nearby or in the distance. But the sound was always present, like the chirping of birds early in the morning. Initially, I was in a constant state of alertness—ready at any moment to hit the floor. That soon gave way to curiosity about how near to my location the fighting was taking place, and then to the sound becoming a part of daily living. Aside from those inconveniences life went on, and things that were abnormal became normal.

I worked arduously to re-establish a fully functioning office amid the confusion of where we lived and toiled. The staff, local and foreign, worked well together with the occasional hiccups due mainly to culture. I was asked, several times, to arbitrate disputes between colleagues. One such incident involved someone from Fiji who hung a poster of a pig being roasted over a slow-burning fire in his office. He was homesick for the ordinary pleasures of his homeland and was hurt, and somewhat insulted, when his Somali colleagues refused to enter his office. He was oblivious to their pain, and their being insulted in the presence of an unclean animal, albeit a picture of the animal. My colleague was truly apologetic, and destroyed the poster as soon as he realized what had caused the problem. Discussing clan affiliations with a Somali was also taboo, unless he or she detected a genuine desire to understand the intricacies of the clan system.

So the office functioned. We worked from 0800 to 1500 hours officially, but most times we were in the office during the afternoon and evening. There was very little else to do except work, go home and then work some more. We ate, slept, relaxed and did all the ordinary things in communal security. Banditry was rife, not only as far as vehicles were concerned, but with any property, whether they were nailed down or not. All compounds had guards who worked on rotating shifts over a 24-hour period. Actually, robbery was not only directed at foreigners, but Somalis robbed Somalis. Abandoned houses and compounds were taken over by members of other clans. Even occupied dwellings were sometimes invaded, and the people living there were killed or driven from their homes. There was lawlessness and the criminal element that existed before the civil war, took advantage of the situation under the guise of:

"We are at war."

International personnel were forced to live together in harmony or misery. Living in misery implied that some people could not get over their cultural differences and sometimes those with authority lauded it over their subordinates. Every now and then there was respite from the monotony by visiting other colleagues in their homes for drinks and meals. Those visits were usually restricted to daylight hours because it was dangerous to travel the streets at night. Foreigners also found relief in the occasional trips to Nairobi to break the tedium, and to be reminded that people lived normal lives in other places.

It was also a pleasure to sample the culinary diversity of Nairobi. Everything that was missing in Somalia was available, even cherries, apples, grapes and other fruits. Being in Nairobi and other cities was better than enduring the monotony of meals served at breakfast, lunch, and dinner in Mogadishu. Pasta was an everyday staple with tomato sauce that was so acidic most people, me included, developed some aversion to tomato sauce long after leaving Somalia.

There were healthy foods, of course, such as papaya, bananas and honey, served every day at breakfast with eggs, toast and coffee. Lunch usually consisted of goat meat, that was boiled to soften it before being stewed, was served with rice and a variety of cooked vegetables. Raw vegetables were taboo. Dinner was pretty much the same as lunch with the occasional grilled fish. Most people lost weight within a few months of arrival in Somalia only to put it back on after a few days in Nairobi.

Then, there was the drinking. Liquor was readily available, and became even more so with the establishment of a few stores within the confines of the United Nations compound. Name it, and most likely it was on the shelves or could be obtained within a few days. There were all kinds of spirits, not only by type but also by brand, including JW black and red, White Horse, Jack Daniels. Gin, and beer, liquors, wines, brandies and cigarettes were also available. There was no stinting on exotic foods like caviar. We had access to cheese, crackers, chocolate, and candies. One store also carried a wide range of electronic equipment, including cameras, wrist watches, short wave radios, VCRs, televisions, and stereos. Store shelves were also lined with jewelry, perfumes and colognes, and were sold at prices that were comparable to the same items in the Nairobi duty-free shops.

The good things notwithstanding, the stresses of living in Somalia carried with it some negative results brought on by indulgence and excesses. Those things affected both those who drank too much before being assigned to Somalia, and those who were unable to bear the stress without some kind of stimulant to endure the pressure of daily living.

Some people, who had never fired a weapon in their lives, began walking around with pistols strapped to their sides. When that was officially banned, they began carrying concealed weapons. Toting a weapon was not only relegated to pistols as firearms of all types were readily available in the local market. Some people, of the Rambo ilk, bought AK47s and M16s, although possessing weapons of any kind was banned.

There were a few incidences that could have had disastrous consequences. On one occasion someone, in a drunken stupor, discharged an Ml6 within the confines of his quarters. Fortunately, the bullet exited his room without causing bodily harm to anyone. It passed through a nearby cabin and destroyed a refrigerator. A few weeks later someone designed a T-shirt with a cartoon character, shaped like a refrigerator and adorned with arms held high with the caption:

"Don't shoot."

A few days before my arrival in Somalia, UNDP had received information that a village, some 200 miles south of Mogadishu, was on the brink of being obliterated by starvation. It was dangerous to go to that area because marauding gangs were known to be operating there. However lives were at stake, so humanitarian consideration outweighed the dangers, and a mission was organized to go to the village and help those living there.

It consisted of four vehicles, two of which carried armed guards, food, water and medicines. One vehicle had enough fuel for the return trip, and the other had four officials, including two doctors, a nurse and a disaster assessment officer. The team had taken trips like that many times before. Most times, there were satisfying results after rendering assistance to those who would have been lost to disease and starvation if the team had not intervened. But sometimes help arrived too late, and people died, or the rescue team found villages that were deserted.

The mission had taken to the road when disaster struck. It had to be abandoned due to a near-fatal accident that destroyed one of the vehicles, and injured several of the guards. The accident occurred some fifty miles south of Mogadishu as the vehicles sped along the road trying to reach their destination before nightfall. The UNDP convoy was making good time when they saw another convoy approaching them. The road, though unpaved, was wide enough to allow vehicles to pass with room to spare. On that occasion, the lead vehicle in the other convoy swerved and hit the UNDP vehicle head on. At the time of impact, the vehicles had slowed down and were only traveling about 20 miles per hour. The impact, even at that speed, was enough to destroy one vehicle, and threw one driver and two guards clear of the vehicles in which they were traveling.

The other vehicles, in both convoys, were traveling at a safe distance from each other and were not affected by the collision. Both sides blamed the other for the accident, and only the negotiating skills of one of the doctors prevented a gun battle from erupting. It was fortunate also that the crews of the two convoys belonged to related sub-clans and were not on opposing sides of the conflict. The doctors immediately attended to the injured. Most of them had lacerations on arms, faces and legs. One guard's leg was fractured. The doctors applied a makeshift splint, and while they worked on the injured man, other members of the team loaded the supplies and equipment onto the undamaged vehicles. The mission returned to Mogadishu having lost one vehicle and some of the supplies.

A few days later as the team was preparing to resume the mission, information was received that the targeted village had been abandoned. UNDP never found out what happened to the people, and why the sudden departure. The assumption was that the villagers must have been informed of an imminent invasion of their area, and since their lives were more important than possessions, they had left with only the things they could carry. UNDP was making other plans when news was received that had momentous implications for the entire humanitarian efforts in Somalia.

By November 1992, the dire situation in Somalia could not be ignored by the United States any longer. Some 60% of humanitarian aid was stolen by armed gangs allied to the two warring factions. After being prodded by members of Congress and other top ranking government officials, President George H. W. Bush decided to intervene by providing military support, for humanitarian purposes. The decision was made just a few days before Thanksgiving when President Bush was in the process of handing over the reins of Government to President Elect, William Clinton.

In his speech to the nation on December 4, 1992, President Bush said that the U.S. was not the world's policeman. However, he continued, there were some situations where the U.S. could help. America had the capacity and the global reach to send troops to such distant places like Somalia, quickly and efficiently. That ability had the potential to save of thousands of lives. The intervention was to be carried out under the banner "Operation Restore Hope."

The U.N. Security Council welcomed the proposed United States intervention and saw it as a plus in restoring order in Somalia. There was, however, a consensus among U.N. Member States that Somalia's debacle demanded more than providing humanitarian aid. They felt that any intervention should be coupled with disarmament- -a vital component in restoring peace. Members of the U.N. Security

Council who were intimately involved in what was happening in Somalia knew that, so long as weapons were easily available, peace was an elusive dream.

Although there was the absence of the disarmament component in the proposed intervention, the news of the U.S. involvement was welcomed by humanitarian agencies on the ground in Somalia. UNDP and other organizations were anxious for their teams to go to several areas in the countryside where people were known to be in need of food and medical services. The overall situation was still chaotic, but lives were at stake, so action had to be taken as soon as was possible to alleviate suffering.

The mission, that had to be aborted because of the accident, weighed heavily on the mind of the UNDP Representative. Anyone who had seen a village in distress, and possessed even the slightest concern for human suffering, was forever touched by such an experience. The Representative had seen such suffering, not only in the countryside, but was reminded on a daily basis of what was going on all over Somalia. The refugee camps that he passed on a daily basis, were constant reminders that there was work to be done without an end in sight.

While I had not been on an evaluation or a rescue mission, I had seen enough in the camps in Mogadishu to know Somalis were in dire circumstances. The atmosphere in the office also told the story of how impotent people felt in not being able to reach all those who were in need. The children were upper most in the minds of aid workers, both local and international. There were too many orphans, too many who had lost relatives and friends needlessly, at least in their immature minds.

However, although most were anxious to resume their mission, travel was postponed, for security reasons, pending the arrival of the Americans. There was no need to place lives in jeopardy when help was on the way. Help they all knew would lessen their burden of being attacked by criminal elements as they travel Somalia's dusty and dangerous roads.

2

Restore Hope

"Hope is a waking dream"
Aristotle

At the same time the U.S. announced its intervention in Somalia, the United Nations appointed a new Special Representative (SR) for the country. Hikmat Kitani, an Iraqi, was selected to replace the outgoing Special Representative, Mohammed Sahnoun. He had tendered his resignation because he was disappointed with his inability to bring any meaningful change in Mogadishu and other parts of the country. Under new leadership, the administrative component of UNOSOM would continue to be headed by the Special Representative while an American would take the lead role with regard to the military activities.

The U.N. suggested that disarmament should form an integral part of the U.S. initiative. However the U.S. stated, unequivocally, that relieving Somalis of their arms and ammunition was out of the question. President Bush also said that American soldiers would be home in time for President Clinton's inauguration in January 1993. That statement, in itself, precluded any possibility that the U.S. would become involved in disarmament. However, most U.N. officials, particularly those who had seen the carnage first hand, did not believe that intervention, on humanitarian grounds along, would be sufficient to stabilize the country.

Even so, the plans for Operation Restore Hope, approved by the United Nations Security Council, went into effect on December 3, 1992. Its mandate was to protect food and medical supplies and ensure that they were delivered to the distribution centers throughout the country. The military part of the intervention, The Unified Task Force (UNITAF), was under the command of Lieutenant Gen Robert B. Johnston. UNITAF had the authority to use any means needed, including military might, if that became necessary. The Force comprised some 37,000 military and civilian personnel. 25,000 were from the United States and the balance from 27 countries, including Bangladesh, Canada, France, Italy, Kuwait, Nigeria, Tunisia, Turkey and The United Kingdom.

The first contingent to arrive in Somalia was from the United States. There was the expectation of conflict, particularly from Aidid's militia, since they stood to lose much of their revenue from looting food and medical supplies. The anticipated conflict did not materialize as the first contingent of U.S. Marines landed, without incident, on a Mogadishu beach on December 9, 1992. A few colleagues and I were on the rooftop of our residence early that morning, and, as the mist rose from the sea, we saw the first wave of marines hit the beach. Instead of hostile militias' intent on keeping the marines off Somali soil, they were met by journalists from all over the world, intent on reporting the auspicious occasion.

Soon after the arrival of the Americans, and other forces comprising UNITAF, there was a dramatic improvement in the delivery of food and medical supplies. The roads became safer to travel, even after sundown, and there was less evidence of weapons on display in the streets. The discharge of heavy artillery seemed to have been a figment of our imaginations. One day as I was going to a meeting, I noticed a scene that repeated itself in the weeks that followed. French soldiers, on patrol with American soldiers, were confiscating weapons from Somalis. The Americans, on the other hand, did nothing to disarm the Somalis. The American policy not to be involved in disarmament was ill advised. It was not long before the weapons, they refused to confiscate, were turned against them.

Nevertheless, UNITAF did an excellent job in quelling the violence, and halting the deaths of people from starvation. UNITAF reached its full complement of 37,000 military and civilian personnel by mid-January 1993. Engineers attached to various units repaired roads, bridges and even constructed buildings to help in the humanitarian efforts.

Even as the security situation improved, there were political considerations that played a critical role in the months after the inauguration of President Clinton. Although the President publicly supported the U.N. mandate in Somalia, he was instrumental in weakening its efforts by announcing, soon after his inauguration, a reduction in the number of U.S. forces from 25,000 to 4,200. Although the cut was to take effect in May 1993, when a revised U.N. initiative, UNOSOM II, was scheduled to start, President Clinton's policy on Somalia would prove to be detrimental to the humanitarian efforts in Somalia. However before the factions realized they could take advantage of a weakened military presence in the country, life was assuming some measure of normalcy. Markets reopened; travel became more common, and there was even some hope of restarting a Somali national police force. Improved security emboldened UNOSOM and other humanitarian agencies, to resume their work of traveling to areas that were affected by violence and famine.

One of those missions headed by UNDP took to the road in late January 1993. As with previous missions, the rescue and evaluation team included two doctors, a nurse, a disaster-relief expert, four guards and drivers to man four vehicles. The vehicles were loaded up with medical supplies, food, tents and sufficient fuel for the return trip of some 400 miles. The trip was uneventful until the mission was a few miles from their destination.

A member of the team reported that there was an eerie silence as they approached the village. Nothing moved though a slight wind wafted through the trees. There was no movement as if the trees and shrubs or even the animals, that they knew to be nearby in the underbrush, had conspired to maintain silence. Was this a premonition of what was to come? The team was silent forming a reluctant partner in the conspiracy.

At that very moment, as if being directed by a choirmaster, the group looked up in unison scanning the sky for some movement, some form of life. However, the birds had deserted the area leaving the group, the only moving, living beings that dared to invade that place at that time. Even their psyche took their cue from some unknown hand because to a man fear gripped them; fear of the unfamiliar or fear of consciously knowing what they would encounter just a few miles down that dusty road.

The mission arrived in the village and saw the horror unfold before them. Almost the whole village of some 150 souls had deserted the village except for five villagers who had succumbed to starvation, disease and death. It seemed that those who could had left quickly. Domestic animals and chickens had disappeared. Not one grain of corn or a bunch of bananas could be found. It was as if a swarm of locusts had passed through eating everything in its path. But, the invaders were people who ate or stole anything of value that lay in their path. They also killed on a whim, to settle old scores, committing genocide as they combed the countryside.

One member of the team came across the most devastating sight he had ever encountered in his twenty-odd years of relief work. It was that of a mother cradling her young; both curled up in a fetal position as death came and claimed them. Not one member of the team could describe their experience without tears and vivid recollections of what they saw that day. No one even tried to hazard a guess as to why those who died had remained. There was no evidence of violence on the bodies only the gaunt features resulting from starvation; skin stretched tightly over the bones.

The flesh on some corpses had started to decompose and had attracted bugs of all kinds. The smell of decomposing flesh was overwhelming. It was difficult for anyone, who had not seen a dead body before, to absorb the shock of seeing five bodies at the same time. The visual was too much, so they left the village as they had found it. The lateness of the hour increased their desire to leave and find shelter for the night elsewhere. Their intention was to return to the village, early the next day, to bury the dead.

One of the guards knew the area quite well, so he directed the team to a village that was some twenty miles off to the east. Inexplicable, the village and its seventy inhabitants had not been scourged as the one they had just left. The people in the village were without adequate food for some time. However, they had managed to survive the devastation that affected most villages in the area.

It was late in the evening when the team arrived in the village, exhausted mentally and physically. They had not thought about food, except for crackers and water as they traveled the dusty unpaved roads. Even if they were so inclined, food was the farthest thing from their minds. The villagers had offered to share their meager resources with the team, but no one could even think about eating at a time like that. The horrors of what they had seen twenty miles away were still very much on their minds. They unloaded the vehicles and presented the food and some of the medical supplies to the chief. He and the villagers were most grateful for the unexpected largess. They were also thankful when the doctors offered to examine anyone who was suffering from any ailment. Although they were fatigued, both mentally and physically, the doctors attended to the villagers' needs as best they could.

Early the following day one of the drivers took six men to the abandoned village to bury the dead. The task was tedious and each grave took longer than usual to dig. The earth was tough because of the prolonged drought, but the men applied their considerable strength and determination to give the dead a decent burial. When they returned, the team took their leave of the villagers for the return trip to Mogadishu. The ride was rough and most uncomfortable, but no one complained. Their discomfort was less important than to be on the road after dark.

It took several days for members on the team to sit with others in the office and report on what they had accomplished. Some staff from two other humanitarian agencies were also present at the meeting to exchange information. A few days after the meeting, the team took some much-needed rest and recuperation in Nairobi.

During the first week of March 1993, a retired United States Admiral, Jonathan Howe, was appointed, to the post of Special Representative, to replace the outgoing Hikmat Kitani. Admiral Howe was tasked with overseeing the transition from UNOSOM to UNOSOM II. Shortly after Howe took up his duties, the U.N. Security Council passed Resolution 814 which changed UNOSOM's mandate to include re-constituting a government comprising leaders from the various clans. The revised mandate also charged UNOSOM with establishing and maintaining an inventory of heavy artillery, supervising the operations to clear mines; and assisting in repatriating refugees from camps in Kenya and Ethiopia. The revised mandate was doomed to failure because the U.N. did not have the resources, financially or militarily, to implement such a grandiose plan.

In May 1993, UNOSOM II took over from UNOSOM. Its military, referred to as Peacekeepers, was made up of soldiers from the same countries that supported UNITAF. The Peacekeepers were under the command of Lieutenant General Çevik Bir (Turkey) and comprised 28,000 military and civilian police personnel. UNOSOM II was ill-prepared for its new role on several fronts. Scaling back on the number of American soldiers, with their well-trained cohesive units, with quality weapons, was a bad idea. As the number of American troops was reduced from 25,000 in January 1993 to 4,200 by May 1993, the ability to respond quickly and decisively to any threat was removed. The clans soon realized they had the upperhand, and gradually reverted to what they had been doing prior to the implementation of Operation Restore Hope.

Civilian support for carrying out the mandate never reached its required strength and, therefore, obstructed implementing parts of the mandate such as the repatriation of refugees. The expertise of senior officials with special technical skills to organize government departments, and train recruits, in a country that was without a government for some three years, was also lacking.

Another factor that impeded progress and, indeed, exacerbated tensions between UNOSOM II and Aidid, was the newly appointed SR Howe's misguided notion to treat Aidid as the enemy. Howe thought that his best option was to isolate Aidid because he was the most powerful warlord, and continued to express his opposition to the U.N's presence at every turn. Howe violated a fundamental principle of peacekeeping, "treat all combatants the same". Do not single anyone out for special treatment---whether good or bad.

In addition to basic operational procedures, Howe was advised by UNDP Consultant, John Drysdale, that it was a bad idea to try to isolate Aidid. In the Somali context, such action by outsiders was considered as an attempt to destroy the clan itself, not Aidid. Under such circumstances, even those members of Aidid's clan who were opposed to him, and were working behind the scene to depose him, would get behind him to prevent the clan from becoming extinct. Unfortunately, neither the principles of peacekeeping, nor the consultant's advice was followed with disastrous consequences.

However, before the implementation of UNOSOM II, there was a subtle deterioration in security that was, somehow, attributed to Admiral Howe. A few of the warring factions, headed by Aidid, tested UNITAF's resolve in light of the planned withdrawal of most of the U.S. soldiers. Some groups even tried, and were successful in some instances, to hijack food and medical supplies between the port and the distribution centers.

A few weeks after Admiral Howe arrived in the country, I was at the airport to check on a shipment of medical supplies for our Medical Center, and to meet two political advisors who had just arrived in the country. We had lunch in a small restaurant at the airport while we discussed their mission and the general situation in the city. We were so pre-occupied with our conversation that we did not notice dark clouds were gathering on the horizon to the west of the airport.

3

A Different Place

*"A little learning is a dangerous thing.
Drink deep, or taste not the Pierian Spring:
There shallow draughts intoxicate the brain,
and drinking largely sobers us again."
Alexander Pope*

The airport was not one of my favorite places because of the prevalence of weapons on display that un-nerved me. However I had a job to do, so I disregarded my discomfort and met with my colleagues. After lunch and our discussion, I assigned two vehicles to transport them to their residence. I then went to a dispatcher to pick up the medical supplies and check on a shipment of diesel we were expecting. There was some kind of labor unrest in Mombasa, Kenya that affected ships bound for Somalia

As I left the dispatcher's office, I saw the dark clouds over the sea and knew for a certainty that rain was imminent. I had been told that it never rained in Mogadishu. There were times when rain threatened, but that was all; it threatened; no water coming down from the sky. However, that day it rained, with no wind and trees swaying under its onslaught, just rain as tons of water were dumped on the city. It had not rained in Mogadishu, not even a drizzle, for several years. As a result, the parched earth gobbled up the rain, though it came down in torrents. In other places, the ground was as hard as a rock, so the water turned into rivulets. They flowed in streams forming small pools at the base of some buildings that blocked their path.

The rain was not the only thing that caused some level of concern to everyone, but included the sudden noise from heavy artillery being discharged. The daily barrage had ceased just after the arrival of UNITAF in December of the past year. I thought that the use of artillery was a thing of the past. I was mistaken, and puzzled, wondering why the breach in the agreement between the clans to cease from shelling each other.

It seemed as if the barrage increased in intensity as I stood there, looking at the rain, and trying to judge how far away the exchange of artillery fire was taking place. I saw flashes of light to the east of the airport, followed by booms as cannons were discharged. The flash of light and the booming sound simulated lightning and thunder. If I did not know better, I would have thought that the city was being treated to a thunderstorm.

When I first arrived in Mogadishu, I had met a pilot, of a small commuter jet, Sam Goddard. He had been quite talkative and I had taken a liking to him. Now here he was at the airport having just flown in from Nairobi. Although he did not show it at the time, he was alarmed by the sound of artillery. He was a Vietnam veteran who had learned to fly helicopters during the war, and had flown some really dangerous missions. After the war, Sam had returned to college to complete his studies that were rudely interrupted in 1966 when he was drafted into the army. He could have requested a deferment, because he was in college, but he felt his country needed him so off to the Army he went. Sam had fallen in love with flying; not in conflict situations, but in circumstances that afforded some leisure.

"This is not good", Sam said addressing his copilot. "The rain is a bad omen for me. Besides that, I would not like to spend an overnight in this place. If this rain does not let up in the next fifteen minutes we will have no choice but to bed down for the night."

The runway was slowly turning into a river, and that was what spurred on Sam's anxiety as his eyes kept scanning the sky for any sign of a let up in the deluge. But what he saw was not promising. As we watched, wave upon wave of dark moisture laden clouds rolled by dumping their load on the city as more clouds seemed to be forming on the horizon.

It was only 1500 hours, yet it was so dark it seemed as if night had set in. That condition served to heighten Sam's anxiety. His unease was slowly rising and spurred on his well-known temper. His anger could be unleashed on anyone or anything that threatened his authority, his peace of mind or his manhood. Sam could not cajole the elements, so he felt powerless and turned his rage on his co-pilot.

"What in God's name were you thinking when you arranged this flight?" Sam remarked in a menacing voice.

"You had better get off my case immediately," retorted Gil Pasqual. "You know that I don't arrange flights. We are at the beck and call of our employer. We fly when they say we fly. In any case, who would have known that this squall would set in? We have been flying between Nairobi and Mogadishu for a little over a year, and it never rained until today."

The silence between the two men was as palpable as the patter of rain on the tin roofs of the buildings. It was deafening and would have exploded into recriminations on both sides if it were not for the huge cargo plane that suddenly materialized out of the gloom. The plane landed, and roared down the runway its brakes and reverse thrust were fully applied. It sprayed water in its wake as the pilot used considerable strength and skill to keep the plane steady and on the runway.

At the same time as the plane was speeding down the runway, two five ton trucks appeared and raced towards the plane that had stopped at the other end of the airport. In the semi darkness, we could see sack after sack being dumped from the plane and being loaded onto the trucks.

"What are they doing?" I asked no one in particular. "Whatever they are picking up will be soaked before being loaded on to the trucks."

"The plane is carrying the bi-weekly supply of qat and the sacks are covered with plastic." Sam responded. "I noted the markings on the plane as it sped by. It is coming in from The Yemen and qat is not the only thing that is being imported from that country. It is as if the Somalis do not have enough problems of their own, what with the civil war, no government and famine. Now they are also being courted by fundamentalists. That does not bode well for the country and what the International Community is trying to rectify."

Sam must have seen the blank look on my face, indicating that I did not have a clue about what he had just said.

"The first thing you must learn in this part of the world, or anywhere for that matter, but particularly here, is that you do not give away your feelings. Keep a poker face when dealing with anyone otherwise people will see your expressions as weakness that **will** be exploited." Sam's demeanor was one of concern as he spoke again.

"It's quite obvious that you do not have any idea about what is going on and that what I just said was Greek to you. Your employer is remiss in not briefing its staff on essential issues pertaining to work and life in this place. I can tell you know nothing about qat and the tentacles that are slowly, but surely being used to rope in this country into a broad coalition of religious zealots. I think I know the answer to the question I am going to ask, but I will ask it even so. How much do you know about the fundamentalist movement in this part of the world?"

I did not want to appear totally ignorant, so I gave a textbook response referencing Israel and Palestine; the U.S. supporting dictatorships in Egypt, the Yemen, Tunisia and a number of other places in the region. I spoke about Desert Storm, and touched briefly on Al Qaeda. I wanted to show that I knew something about that organization, though there was no evidence they were involved in Somalia, at least not at that time.

Sam looked amused but did not respond at that time. Instead, his attention was focused on the plane that was racing down the runway, this time picking up speed for takeoff. It went pass us with a roar. Just when it seemed as if it would plunge into the sea that formed the eastern boundary of the airport; it lifted off the ground, swaying ever so slightly in the heavy downpour and vanishing from sight.

"That is one crazy, daring, idiot of a pilot, with incredible skills." Sam remarked.

The words preceding pilot were not complimentary in our vocabulary, but apparently in Sam's lingo, it meant that the pilot had extraordinary abilities.

"There must be a really good reason why he chose to take such risks rather than wait for morning to take off. It was bold enough to land in such conditions, but to take off?" Sam mused. "Perhaps there is a price on his head in Mogadishu, or he found it more acceptable to risk life and limb rather than bed down for the night."

Sam was quiet for what seemed like a long time. He was deep in thought about what he had just witnessed. Maybe he was considering taking off himself, but he knew that was not going to happen. He believed his employers would penalize him if he were responsible for placing their most reliable means of transportation, in and out of Mogadishu, in jeopardy.

However, Sam was thinking about other things as we stood there. He was contemplating how much of his knowledge about Somalia he should disclose to me. As an American, he understood all too well the dangers of just being American in Somalia. The dangers were not manifested in the casual dealings with Somalis in general. As a matter of fact, he felt that there was a kind of benevolent tolerance the Somalis showed to Americans.

They were considered friends who helped during the war with Ethiopia in 1977-1978. Prior to the war with Ethiopia, Somalia was allied to the Soviet Union while Ethiopia, through Emperor Haile Selassie, was in the American camp. After the Emperor had been deposed in September 1974, the Somalis took advantage of the turmoil in Ethiopia. Three years later they launched an attack to regain the Ogaden region of Ethiopia that Somalia had always considered a part of its territory. Somalia was defeated by Ethiopia, but during the conflict, the Soviets became the allies of Ethiopia, and America became Somalia's benefactor, providing the arms Somalia needed to continue their fight with Ethiopia.

Although Somalis, in general, regarded Americans as friends, the problem was with the fundamentalists, the ones who had been converted to the ideology of radical Islam. They bought into the paranoia of America being the enemy of Islam. They were the ones who had introduced an element of hatred and hostility towards Americans, and were against what America stood for.

Sam knew I was from Belize, but he felt I could be mistaken for an American by those bent on doing harm to Americans. With those thoughts in mind, Sam concentrated once more on the weather and his plans for the night.

"There is no way we'll be able to fly back to Nairobi tonight," Sam said as he turned towards me. "I hope you have some good scotch or brandy in your larder. This will be a long night for me, and I will need some help to fall asleep."

"We have room in the Residence for both of you. And yes I have some scotch in my room."

My answer was quick and inviting. I had hoped Sam and his co-pilot would have had to spend the night. Sam was an interesting man, and I felt I could learn a lot from this cranky, but likable, fellow.

"No need to hang around here any longer. It is really getting dark, and I would prefer to be in the safety of the U.N. Residence at night rather than on the street." Sam seemed preoccupied as he spoke, not because he was afraid of being in Mogadishu, but with some concern for what the future held.

Without saying another word, we started towards the vehicle that was parked a few yards from where we stood. Dusk had settled on the city by that time. The driver and guards in our vehicle seemed a little on edge, nervously looking around as we drove to our residence. I asked the driver, who spoke English extremely well, why they appeared to be worried. He just shrugged his shoulders and said that there was nothing out of the ordinary. There were rumors about a clash between two sub-clans that could erupt at any time and in any place.

A few days before, a child of about eight years was playing in the street when he was hit by a car driven by a Marehan clansman. The child, who died on the spot, was Habar Gidir. Relatives of the child, who were standing nearby, witnessed the accident and immediately gave chase since the vehicle did not stop but sped away from the scene. The driver of the vehicle that hit the child knew that he would have been killed if he had gotten out of his vehicle to ascertain whether the child was hurt or had died. That was the beginning of yet another feud that added to the war weary city.

In the days before the civil war and the conflict that followed had deteriorated into outright clan violence, the elders of both clans would have been the arbitrators to determine who was fault. They would also have been the ones to establish the level of compensation that was to be paid. The elders haggled but always came up with solutions. However, those days were long gone so the gun took the place of arbitration.

That was the reason for concern and the fact that such clashes had increased dramatically during the past two week. Renewed fighting, regardless of the origin, would indicate that UNITAF was losing its grip on making the country secure.

We arrived at the residence and were just in time for supper. The table was set, and some people had already gathered around sipping drinks, smoking and talking. There was no need for introductions because everyone had met Sam and Gil at some time, so appropriate pleasantries were exchanged. I noticed some tension, slight but evident, between Sam and one person in the room.

Walif Hamza was on assignment with UNOSOM as a political adviser. He hailed from the Sudan, was a rabid Islamist and hated anyone or anything American. His hatred included those he perceived to be in league with American policies. It did not matter to him if his assumptions were reasonable or not. His perception or evaluation of a person's affiliation was enough for him to designate that person an acolyte of the great prostitute. That meant there could be no friendship between him and anyone he believed to be complicit in carrying out or agreeing with American foreign policies.

Sam talked about Walif later in the evening when we were discussing Somalia and what was happening in the country. Something that escaped Sam, in his assessment of Walif, was that he had no problems with American women. Their association with, or involvement in American foreign policies, was of no importance to him. Walif was a womanizer. Much later on I had a conversation with him about his unabashed hatred of Americans, except for the women. He told me that women were weak vessels and were innocent participants in the evil being perpetrated by the American Government. He made no mention of the fact that women, regardless of their color, race or creed, were the great passion in his life.

Sam and I talked well into the night. Actually Sam spoke, and I listened except for a few questions. He had taken one drink of the twelve-year old scotch that I had produced because, he confessed; he was not a drinking man. More importantly he had to fly back to Nairobi the next day and did not want any alcohol in his system.

He talked about Somalia from way back in antiquity, as he referred to the early days of the Somali Republic, and included features of the Somali culture. How the Republic came into being, and the aftermath was very important factors in what was happening in January 1993. The coup d'état in 1969, the civil war starting in 1990; the ousting of the dictator Siad Barre in January 1991 and the famine that gripped the country were critical pieces in the puzzle that was Somalia. Everything was exacerbated by the clan or family rivalry that took center stage amid the confusion. It was the clan, and by extension the leader of the clan, that spoke for everyone.

The original Somali Kingdom in the Horn of Africa was arbitrarily fragmented into five parts late in the nineteenth century. The Ethiopians conquered the Ogaden around 1890. About the same time, the French colonized a section of the northern part of Somalia, named it Djibouti, while the British granted Protectorate status to an area adjacent to Djibouti, and named it British Somaliland. The Italians, not to be outdone, colonized territory south of British

Somaliland and called it Italian Somaliland. The north eastern corner of Kenya was once an integral part of the Somali Kingdom. It was colonized by the British and became known as the Northern Frontier District.

The fragmentation, which was one piece of the puzzle, had always been a bone of contention for Somalis. It was not surprising, therefore that when independence was granted to the two Somalilands in July 1960 the leaders brought the two territories together and called it the Republic of Somalia. They did not stop there, but made it their mandate to re-unite with the lost territories in Ethiopia, Kenya and Djibouti. As can be imagined, that did not sit well with the governments in those countries.

When Kenya was granted her independence in 1963, Somalis in the Northern Frontier District demanded that the Government of Kenya allowed detachment from Kenya and reunion with the Somali Republic. The demand was denied.

The Ethiopians would not entertain giving up the Ogaden, regardless of what the Somalis said or did; outside of military conquest. It was widely held, by Somali leaders, that Ethiopia was responsible for fueling the fires of discontent among some clans that ignited the Somali civil war in 1990. Their alleged involvement may also have been in retaliation for the Somali invasion of Ethiopia in the 1977-1978 war. Whether those allegations were true or not, the civil war precluded any further moves by Somalia to reunite the Ogaden with the Somali Republic.

Friendly relations were maintained with Djibouti, but the French was always wary of the Somali government because of its well-publicized efforts to bring all Somalis into the union. As a matter of fact, Somalia did not sign the 1963 Organization of African Unity (OAU) Charter because one of its guiding principles was that members must respect the borders that were inherited from the colonial masters.

Without expanding any further on the geopolitical problem of Somalia, Sam talked about unrest in the country that was exacerbated by outside influences. There was a real problem with Islamists who had gained a foothold in several areas of the country. In the beginning, they were influential in Bosasso, but were ousted by the major clan in the area, the Majerteyn. They thought that the Islamists were trying to take control of the area. After being driven out of Bosasso, the Islamists had spread their tentacles to other parts of the country. They had a problem getting a foothold in Mogadishu because of their strict injunction against cigarettes, qat, music and educating women.

Most foreigners, particularly those involved in security, believed that the Islamists, from all over the Arab world, were trained at camps in the Yemen. They were well financed and guided by Iran, and to some extent, by the Sudan. Sam did not mention Walif in any of his references to the Sudan, and Walif's involvement in their work in Somalia. Sam intimated, however, that Walif was some sort of agent for the Iranians. He did not go into any details about his source of information, but suggested that I should be aware of forces at work to destabilize the country even further.

I had not heard about qat before Sam told me about it at the airport. He explained that qat was a narcotic that Somalis, mostly men, used extensively. Qat is a green leafy plant, Sam explained, that is chewed and is kept in a ball between the cheek and gum, like chewing tobacco. The scientific assessment of the drug, also spelled khat in other places, and tchat in Ethiopia, is that it is addictive with excessive use, causes insomnia, stress and depression. Notwithstanding the clinical, negative aspects of the drug, Somalis swear by its euphoric effects. Somalis believe that their poets produced their best works while under its influence. While drinking alcohol was forbidden on religious grounds, their religion turned a blind eye to the mind altering effects of qat.

After Sam had gone to bed, I reflected on the valuable information he had given me, and made a mental note that I should learn more about the subjects he had introduced. I was sure that it was not Sam's intention to make me feel like an ignoramus, but that is exactly how I felt as I crawled into bed, exhausted, trying to sort out all the information that was crammed into my overloaded brain. The feeling of inadequacy was reminiscent of Angola and my quest to supplement my only language, English with Portuguese. Most people in the office spoke at least three languages and switched from one to the other with ease. As I laid there trying to recall some Portuguese words and phrases, for no good reason, I fell into a fitful sleep.

I woke at daybreak the next morning, my mind still in a whirl. I tried to remember every detail of my conversation with Sam, and what John Drysdale had told me about Somalis the first day I arrived in the country. One thing was for sure; I had to get as much background information as possible on what happened to have created such a mess. What was it in the psyche of these people that allowed the exercise of such callousness and brutality one to another? They killed, and maimed each other even as they boasted about their lineage. They brag about their homogeneous society, all speaking the same language, and all worshiping Allah with one voice, albeit in different Mosques. And yet, the devastation of Somalia caused by Somalis, and their behavior one towards the other was hard for me to understand.

As I recalled my discourse with John Drysdale, an incident came to my mind that occurred the day after my arrival in Nairobi, Kenya en route to Somalia. On that occasion, I decided to remain in Nairobi for two days before taking the connecting flight to Mogadishu. I had friends in Nairobi, and we had arranged to meet the day after my arrival. As I walked to our rendezvous, I saw a skeleton on legs coming towards me. I had seen pictures of starving human beings, reduced to skin stretched over bones in print and on television, but never in person. The skeleton was bent, like an old man, using a walking stick to assist him as he took one step after another, his head was out of proportion to his body. As he drew nearer, I noticed flies hovering around his mouth to extract the moisture that gathered there.

I assumed he was one of the thousands of Somalis, who had escaped the famine in Somalia and had walked; God knows how many miles, to find refuge. Without thinking of my next move, I stopped him and asked where he had come from and where he was going. He looked at me quizzically, obviously not understanding a word I had said. I then looked around and saw a group of four or five people standing nearby observing me and the boy. I beckoned them over thinking, correctly, from their features that they were Somalis.

A member of the group confirmed that the boy was Somali. His name was Abdul Mohamad and was from one of the refugee camps on the Somali/Kenya border. He had walked and hitch-hiked for hundreds of miles to escape the violence in the camp. I offered to get him to the Nairobi Hospital for treatment, but the spokesman of the group told me that they would take care of Abdul and would see that he received whatever treatment he needed.

The group had taken Abdul to a nearby restaurant and, after determining what he wanted to eat, placed the order and continued to ply him with questions about his travels. I had followed them into the restaurant and suggested that no food should be given. Instead I said that Abdul should have been taken directly to the hospital where professionals would have taken care of him. I was certainly not an expert in dealing with people who were starving, but common sense dictated that regular food would not be tolerated in such cases. The food was served but after only a spoonful or two or rice and some goat meat Abdul became violently ill. He was taken outside at which time I repeated that I would take Abdul to the hospital. However I was told that he was not my problem, and that the group would take good care of him.

The following day, before leaving Nairobi, I went back to the place where I had encountered Abdul. The area was apparently a hangout for Somalis. True enough, I found the same group of Somalis and when I asked about their charge of the previous day, one of the men told me that they had no idea where he went; he had just left, another member of the group told me. I was about to ask another question when he turned back to the group and continued his conversation that I had, apparently, so rudely interrupted. At least that was how I felt, like an interloper.

That incident was forgotten in the wake of all that happened after my arrival in Somalia. As I took a shower and prepared for another day, I thought about how well John was attuned to Somali conduct and character. I thought about Abdul, the refugee in Nairobi, and wondered if the lack of interest in him, by those who had promised to help, was because he belonged to a different clan. The significant thing apparently was not "**where** he was from but **whom** he was from."

As I walked to the office, just next door from my residence, I was engrossed in my thoughts wondering what the day would bring. What new and unusual event would be brought to my attention? I was not in the office for more than an hour when I became aware of the plight of one of our staff members.

4

The Unprotected

"All cruelty springs from weakness."
Seneca

She came to work that morning disheveled and slightly disoriented with a puffy face and a bruise just below her right temple. This tall and striking woman had seen the viciousness of the civil war, clan warfare, deaths or rather executions of friends and family. Khadija Mohammed lived, like most people, in constant fear—not only for herself but also for her two teenage daughters. Without a male protector, their home was not safe from the criminal elements that looked for opportunities to prey on the defenseless.

Her husband had disappeared a few months earlier, and she was convinced that he had been among the many faceless unknown corpses that littered the city-- who were buried without being identified. She knew her husband, and knowing him she was sure that he had not abandoned them. His daughters were his pride and joy from their births sixteen and fourteen years before he disappeared. As the battle raged around them, the family had tried to escape from the city, but it was too late by the time they made the decision to get away.

The exits from Mogadishu were manned by thugs from one clan or the other. There were rumors of people being killed while trying to escape from the city. So the family had stayed hoping that the conflict would end, and life would return to some level of normalcy. Normalcy never came, and Khadija surmised that her husband was killed in one of the many incidences that occurred in the city on a daily basis. She knew what this meant for herself and her daughters—they were now part of the vulnerable and the unprotected.

Khadija tried her best to keep her daughters off the streets. They were appropriately dressed in accordance with strict Muslim custom when they ventured outside their home. All parts of their bodies were covered except for their eyes. Even so, one of the girls had attracted the attention of a degenerate, a coward who preyed on people who were helpless, especially women. One day, he followed her from the marketplace to her home. He then gathered a few men of the same ilk, and observed the people who lived at that address. It was not long before they, the scum of the earth, determined that there were three females living in the house, without a man, so one night they came calling.

Khadija was absent from work for several days; then finally showed up obviously distraught. At first, she refused to relate what was happening at home, but a few female colleagues convinced her that silence would not help her; relenting, she opened up and told her story. She had spoken in a low and soft voice as she recounted how the thugs came one night and had their way with her and her daughters. They were brutalized, raped repeatedly. Over and over Khadija tried to protect her daughters, but was struck down each time. The first night was torture as the intruders kept up their barbaric assault. With their battered bodies, the women were forced to cook and serve their abusers.

Khadija did not want to leave her home because she felt that her presence would somehow lessen the impact of the assault on her daughters. On the third day, she was instructed, by her abusers, to go to the office since any extended absence would prompt someone to show up at her home to check up on her. She left reluctantly; as a matter of fact, staying at home was not an option. She had to leave with the additional instruction not to say a word of what was happening in her home, to anyone.

A few of Khadija's colleagues empathized with her. At least two of the other women had also lost their husbands in the same manner and, after months of searching for them, had come to the same conclusion that their husbands were dead. The wounds that were inflicted on the women were opened once more, and they all cried together in solidarity with this new victim; however, more so because of the continuing assault Khadija and her daughters were enduring. The most immediate action to take was to assist them to escape from their captors.

Some male colleagues were asked for their input on what was the best way to help Khadija and her daughters. The first proposal was to ask UNITAF to help with the rescue. That proposal was rejected since it would have entailed storming the house, and trying to free the hostages. It was considered too dangerous, because of the possibility that the people, they were trying to save, could be killed. In any case, as bad as the situation was, Khadija would not contemplate placing her daughters in danger of being shot.

Khadija and her family belonged to a Hawiye sub-clan. She believed that the intruders were Darood, but she was not sure. She thought that she had heard one of the men talking about being a distant relative of the deposed President, Siad Barre. That being the case, they were taking a risk being in an area that had opposed the former president. Most of the residents of the area were from the Hawiye Clan and some other clans allied to it.

One of the men in the office, Ali Jamal, was a hot head and, immediately after hearing about Khadija's plight, offered to accompany her home to speak with her captors. His idea was that, if he showed that the women were not really alone, he could convince the intruders to leave. Ali's mother was Darood, and if Khadija's guess were right, he would be able to relate to the intruders through their clan affiliation. Not one person in the office agreed that was the best available option. But Ali convinced his coworkers that his plan could work.

Ali's assertions were wrong. That night as he tried to reason with the thugs he was beaten to within an inch of his life and thrown out of the house. The men who assaulted him also said that if he tried to intervene again he would be shot on the spot. He turned up for work the next day bruised and battered, but more determined than before to rescue the women. I had seen Khadija the day she came to the office and the flurry of activities around her. I was anxious to find out what had happened, but I was reluctant to ask any questions.

When I saw Ali's condition the day after he was assaulted, I knew that something was sorely amiss. This was no coincidence; two unrelated staff were assaulted within days of each other was no chance occurrence. At first Ali would not divulge what was going on. He believed that he needed Khadija's permission to disclose what had happened since their stories were linked. But, when he went to look for her, he was told that she had not shown up for work that day. Ali became very agitated and, fearing the worse, he told me what was happening to Khadija, her daughters and what had happened to him when he tried to intervene.

I knew it was useless to seek help from UNITAF. It was not that they would have been unsympathetic. On the contrary, I believed they would have "sent in the cavalry", but I recognized it would have been a nightmare for them to storm Khadija's house. Since I felt that we should take action without delay, I asked my trusted driver, Hassan, what we could do to help. Hassan had already heard what was going on in Khadija's home. He was not therefore surprised at my request.

We discussed the pros and cons of casually going to the house, pretending to be lost and asking for directions. I would not be involved in the reconnaissance mission. That would have been a sure give-a-way. Of course, no one could tell that I was not Somali just by looking at me. I had been mistaken for a Somali on several occasions, but my non-Somali identity had been revealed each time I spoke. That being established, I told Hassan to think about the best approach and get back to me that day.

Hassan disappeared from the office for about four hours, and later that day he came back with a plan. He had used the time to drive around the neighborhood, and at some point, he had parked his vehicle about two blocks from Khadija's house, but at a place where he could observe what was going on. At around 1400 hours, he saw three heavily armed men leave the house got into a vehicle that was parked in front of the house, and drove off. Hassan and his team followed the men to a tea shop that was located about a mile from Khadija's house. Tailing their target was an easy task because there were a number of Technicals on the road, all of them driving at breakneck speeds. There were no speed limit or traffic signs or cops to enforce the laws.

Hassan had returned to his surveillance, and was there for about one hour when the three gunmen returned and entered the house. At that point, Hassan came back to the office and reported to me what he had seen. Khadija had said that there were four men who had taken up residence in her home. Three of them had gone to the tea shop, so it was assumed that one man was left to guard the women. A plan was formulated that day on how best to attempt a rescue.

Hassan believed that the trip to the tea shop took place on a daily basis. The next day he and three heavily armed colleagues took up their position at 1330 hours in the same place as they had done the day before. They wore bullet-proof vests in case shooting broke out. They did not know how the lone gunman in the house would react to some stranger at the door, so the idea was to outflank him by sending one of their own to the back of the house. Radios were turned off so timing was of the utmost importance. Hassan estimated that it should take no more than ten minutes to reach the back of the house using stealth. Luckily, for Hassan's team, the house behind Khadija's was not occupied. They had found that out the day before, when they canvassed the neighborhood. One obstacle had been removed since they did not have to explain why they were trespassing when they had to pass through the adjacent property on their way to rescue the women.

The conjecture was correct. A little past 1400 hours, the same three men exited Khadija's house, got into their vehicle and sped away. Ten minutes later Hassan walked up to the house and rapped on the door. He was confident that his man was at the back of the house, hopefully in a position to help if needed. The door was opened almost immediately, indicating that someone was observing activities in the street, in front of the house.

Khadija was obviously surprised to see Hassan at her door, but the surprise was contained in a slight widening of the eyes; nothing more. She had not been to the office since the day she reported the invasion of her home. She was not even aware that Ali had tried to rescue her and her daughters, and that he was assaulted and warned never to return. There was a commotion in front of her home about two days before, but she had no idea what was going on. There was a rap on the front door, and at that point she and her daughters were locked up in the back room until whoever was at the door had left. She was, therefore, unaware of Ali's visit or the plans to rescue her and her daughters. It was just as well, because the stress of her knowing a rescue was being planned, without having an action time-line, might have alerted her captors that she was expecting something to happen.

Hassan was apologetic as he spoke to Khadija, but at the same time, he strained his eyes to see beyond the crack in the door. The interior of the house was dim; the curtains were drawn, and there was no artificial lighting. Hassan explained that he was looking for his relatives who used to live in the house behind Khadija's. It seemed to him as if the house had been abandoned. He asked if Khadija knew whether the house was empty, or if the occupants had gone away for a few days. She responded that she had been busy at her job during the past two weeks, and had not noticed what had happened to her neighbors. She also said that perhaps her daughters and a visiting cousin might have more information on the subject. With that said she turned, addressed the other occupants of the house and, at the same time, widened the crack in the door.

"Majid, have you seen anyone in the house behind us?" Not wanting to be conspicuous, but apparently more so from being inexperienced in this vicious business, Majid stepped out from the shadows, and came into full view of Hassan. There were no weapons in Majid's hand, but he had a pistol in his waistband.

Hassan immediately brought his hand that was behind his back, into full view so that Majid was staring down the barrel of a Browning 9mm semi-automatic pistol. Majid froze; his jaws dropped, and he started to plead for his life. Hassan told him to place his hands behind his head and not to move a muscle if he valued his life. Hassan took the weapon from Majid's waistband and told Khadija to open the back door. His companion came in and tied Majid up. The women without being told hastily gathered their valuables, and, within less than ten minutes since Hasssan rapped on the door, they were out of the house. They quickly climbed into their vehicle and drove down the road in the opposite direction from the tea shop.

They had driven directly to the office and briefed me on what had happened. There was not enough time to dwell on the well-executed rescue. That would come later when we could go into the details. In the meantime, it was important to get the women out of Mogadishu as soon as was possible. The consensus was that the men, who had invaded Khadija's home, knew that she worked for the United Nations and would come there looking for the women as soon as they found out they had escaped.

Khadija's relatives lived in a village outside Beledweyne, a city about 230 miles to the north-west of Mogadishu. Hassan volunteered to take her and her daughters there. He went to the Water Project, got as much fuel as he needed and left town. I gave Hassan $500 to cover the cost of the trip. I also gave him the name and address of a colleague, who lived in Beledweyne, in case he and his crew needed a place to stay. Two days later Hassan and his team returned to Mogadishu, exhausted both physically and mentally from their experiences. They were given a hero's welcome in the office and were granted two weeks, well deserved, paid leave.

The plight of so many families was reflected in Khadija's story. She never found out for sure what happened to her husband. The assumption was that he had been killed. Much later I received a letter from Khadija thanking me, and all those involved in rescuing her and her daughters. She had also told me that they had been granted refugee status in The Netherlands and were on their way to Europe. I did not respond, simply because she did not provide a return address. However, I received word several months later, through the Somali grapevine that Khadija and her daughters were doing well in their adopted country.

Two days after Khadija and her daughters were spirited out of Mogadishu, one of our guards reported to me that a vehicle, with three and sometimes four men in it, was parked for extended periods about twenty-five yards from the entrance to our office compound. In fact, the presence of the unidentified vehicle was reported to the guards by my cigarette vendor, who had his stand opposite the gate of our compound. Our Street was not a busy one, so the parked vehicle with armed men inside was conspicuous.

No one in the office, except Ali and Khadija, could have identified the men who had invaded Khadijah's home. Ali himself was uncomfortable about the whole affair, and felt certain he would also be targeted. That was a logical conclusion. Therefore, the day following Khadija's flight from Mogadishu, Ali was given an assignment in Nairobi, and he left that same day. I believe the decisive action we took also saved Ali's life because the next day the mysterious vehicle showed up. No one paid any attention, at least overtly, to the vehicle and its occupants and, after a few days, they disappeared just as surreptitiously as they had invaded our space.

Almost nothing surprised any of us. Although there was some improvement in the security situation, I still did not feel safe going out at nights, but took strolls, of a mile or so, during the day. It was liberating to be able to walk the streets, stopping on the way to buy cigarettes, silver jewelry and other commodities at roadside kiosks. However, I was reminded, now and then, that conflict and hostility were a part of the norm. Therefore, when I was threatened with bodily harm by an irate contractor, and six angry young men, about a week after the drama with Khadija, her daughters and Ali, I just took those things in stride.

5

Inshallah (God Willing)

"I shall pass through this world but once. Any good therefore that I can do or any kindness that I can show to any human being, let me do it now. Let me not defer or neglect it, for I shall not pass this way again."
Stephen Grellet

I have tried to live by this philosophy from my youth. Each failure continues to be my constant companion.

The contractor walked into my office, early in the morning, and demanded that I renew an agreement UNDP had with him for transporting staff around Mogadishu. No greetings were exchanged on either side, just two men staring at each other; one with hostility in his demeanor and the other with anxious curiosity. I knew why the contractor was in my office, but his approach signaled a new way of doing business.

"You have no choice but to hire my van to transport your staff." Abdi Othman Ali spoke like a person who was used to have his way.

He also exuded the confidence of a man who had just drawn his shirt aside to show that he was armed. Abdi wanted to intimidate me with his gestures and fixed gaze. He also wanted to convey his determination to use force, if necessary, to accomplish his will.

I had been threatened many times before, but those threats had been made through intermediaries, but this time it was face-to-face. My response came in a calm voice that belied the tremors of fear rippling through my body. The tremors, though real, were not manifested outwardly. Instead, they were felt on the inside, a silent rumbling of my stomach with quivers that were felt at the soles of my feet.

"Your threats are falling on deaf ears particularly since you have contravened one of the conditions of our agreement, and that is, no weapons on the premises," I told the intruder as he sat, uninvited, in the chair facing me.

"Do not lecture me." Abdi countered. "I am not the least bit interested in anything you have to say except to agree to the extension to the contract. Just sign the document in front of you, and I will be on my way. I do not know why you are prolonging the inevitable because, in the end, ***you will*** sign."

Abdi owned three vans that were on lease to organizations within the International Community in Mogadishu. Each van had a driver and two armed men to protect passengers; and keep the vehicle from being hijacked as they navigated the Mogadishu streets. The problem I had with Abdi, and why I had decided not to renew UNDP's contract was that the new driver, who had been assigned to the vehicle about two weeks prior the unscheduled meeting, was unreliable. He could not be found on two occasions when I had to go to UNOSOM, which resulted in my missing two important meetings. There were no problems with the guards, two likable young men, who, though they spoke no English, were amiable and trustworthy. They had proven themselves under fire, and had risked their lives to protect me and another colleague when we landed smack in the middle of a firefight between UNITAF and a contingent of Aidid's militia.

A group of United Nations staffers had been invited aboard a U.S Navy vessel that had sailed into Mogadishu the day before the incident. We had enjoyed a sumptuous meal followed by a movie and drinks. It was pretty late when the party broke up. No one had noticed the time until someone said that it was past midnight, and that we should be returning to our respective residences.

A colleague and I got into our vehicle, discussing the events of the night as we sped through the streets of Mogadishu. Shots rang out as we rounded the corner of the street where we lived. We saw tracer bullets, used by both sides, flashing across the street as the combatants exchanged fire. The guards had shoved me and my colleague to the floor of the vehicle and protected us with their bodies until we were clear of immediate danger. We were both petrified, not having been so close to a fire-fight before although we knew that, at some point, we would be in the wrong place at the wrong time.

Even though no one in my vehicle fired a single shot, Aidid's militia must have assumed that we were part of UNITAF that had engaged them earlier that night. So, they turned their fire on us. Our driver was alert and must have practiced the drill before because as soon as the vehicle came under attack, he placed the vehicle in reverse and sped away from the danger the situation posed. Unfortunately for us, our vehicle hit a parked car and stalled momentarily. At that point, we came under attack once more. As if by instinct, no one said a word, we just prayed to God that the engine would come to life again. Our prayers must have been heard because shortly after the engine stalled it kicked over, and we were speeding away from the conflict. We later found out that the fighting had been going on for about two hours before we arrived on the scene.

As I recalled the incident, I felt a sense of loyalty to Abdi's employees. However, I would not agree to the demand because it was just that, a demand to which, according to Abdi, I had no choice but to comply. An extension to the contract was not a problem. I had already agreed to that with the proviso that the driver, who was with the vehicle before, be brought back in our service.

The minutes ticked by, and I felt that Abdi was growing impatient with my refusal to comply with his demand. He also knew that I would not, under the circumstance, accede to his ultimatum. However, saving face was most important to him; therefore, he sat and stared with some hostility in his eyes. He knew that he could find work, without difficulty, for the guards. So he addressed the topic at hand insisting that the driver had to remain as part of the crew.

"I have made it quite clear to you that I am prepared to renew the contract but that the driver, in question, has to be replaced because I cannot rely on him," I repeated.

Abdi's voice was strident as he told me that I had no choice in the matter, just as he had no choice in retaining the driver.

"He is my sister's husband, and they have eight children. If I fire him, he will not be able to feed his family, and I will be held responsible," Abdi said.

"I understand your predicament." I responded. "Even so, as I told you before, your family's problems are your own and have nothing to do with this office."

I continued the discussion telling him that the decision was his whether the contract would be renewed or not. I also told him to leave my office immediately. Surprisingly, he got up and left after saying, under his breath that he would return the following day with an amended contract.

After Abdi left I felt drained, ready for some respite from the tension he had introduced into my office. I thought about going to my residence to shower and have a drink or two before lunch. I had never taken a drink in the middle of the day before, but believed a drink would have steadied my nerves. As I was about to leave, six young

Somali men walked into my office unannounced and uninvited. Four of them walked directly to a couch that lined the far wall, and sat down without as much as a hello. Their show of disdain for me was deliberate since, under ordinary circumstances, a greeting would have been given in Somali if no one in the group spoke English. Their actions were, no doubt, intended to frighten me.

The left arm of one of the men was heavily bandaged, and his left leg was in a cast. Two of the men had scars on their faces that had only recently healed. They sat staring intently at me without a word being spoken. Something was sorely amiss and once again, within a very short time, fear rippled through my body. But, I said nothing, trying desperately to compose myself, struggling not to show how traumatized I was by their presence. No weapons were visible, but I was sure that one of them carried some sort of weapon, maybe a pistol that could be hidden quite easily.

I returned their stares taking on one of them at a time, making sure I looked at each of them, one by one. Then I found myself staring into the eyes of someone who appeared to be completely devoid of human emotion. It was as if I were staring into an abyss, deep and fathomless; they were eyes of someone who, I believed, could kill without a second thought. It occurred to me that he might have been chewing qat or maybe he was on some other narcotic. I did not know of anyone who had eyes so blank in their normal state; maybe they were the eyes of a born killer. Although I was consumed with a different kind of anxiety, like being in the presence of evil, I held my ground and was only diverted, mercifully, by the voice of one of the intruders. The words were unintelligible, so I held up my hand, got out of my chair, and called through the open door for assistance from a Somali colleague who was hovering in the corridor outside my office.

Ibrahim Abdullah came to my rescue, and asked the group; in general, why they had come to the office. One of the young men answered in halting, but perfect English.

"We were contracted by UNDP to guard a convoy that was taking relief supplies to a village to the south of Mogadishu. We were involved in an accident with another convoy, and have not been able to work since then. UNDP paid for repairs to our vehicle, but we feel that we are entitled to compensation for our injuries."

I knew about the accident and had extensive discussions with the people who were directly involved. I also knew about the efforts the office had made to repair the vehicle. In fact, I was also expecting a request for compensation, so the request was not a surprise. What I did not understand was why they approached me in that manner.

"To the best of my knowledge," I responded, "UNDP has always treated people with respect and fairness. That being the case, why approach me in this manner as if you had to intimidate me into doing what is right?"

The spokesman for the group looked somewhat puzzled as he replied.

"We came here about a week ago to speak with you, but we were turned away at the gate. I returned by myself a few days later but was told you were too busy to see me. We thought you were trying to avoid us so..." and he waved his hand to encompass his colleagues.

I apologized for the misunderstanding, and made a note to speak with the people who had put me and other members of staff in jeopardy. It was not uncommon for Technicals to take matters into their own hands when they felt they were ignored or treated unfairly. In this case, the men were corrected in feeling that their just claim was not being considered.

So the negotiations began, with the leader of the group demanding six weeks' pay as compensation. The counter proposal was for one week, which was rejected outright. We eventually settled on three weeks' pay which, I learned later, was the number of weeks they had decided on even before they came to see me. The group thanked me and left after I promised to have their payment ready within a few days. I would send word to them when they could come to collect it.

My colleague, Ibrahim, who was present while I spoke with the young men, told me that I had handled the negotiations just like a Somali. He was in the habit of quoting Somali proverbs, and this time was no different as he recited a proverb that was suitable for the occasion.

"When negotiating, start by asking for a camel, if you want a goat."

That was good to know since I would have to do quite a bit of contract negotiations during my time in Somalia. I was familiar with the art of negotiating, of course, but the Somali visual illustration of using a goat and a camel was priceless.

As I walked to my residence that evening, after a tension-filled day, I passed a boy sitting in the dusty road. I absentmindedly reached inside my pocket, took out a few Somali Shillings and placed them in his outstretched hand. I gave no further thought about the encounter except for a nagging feeling in the pit of my stomach.

On reflection, I felt I should have stopped and said a kind word to the unfortunate human being instead of doling out money without any human contact. I derided myself for my callousness, but chalked up my behavior to being under stress.

The encounter with the landlord, the men who showed up in my office and the boy were the thoughts that permeated my consciousness as I reached my residence that evening, climbed the stairs to my room and flopped down on my bed totally exhausted. I did not join my colleagues for supper that night, not because of my experiences during the day but from sheer fatigue, and from muddled thoughts of the burden that was Somalia. I fell asleep to the sound of automatic weapons being fired in the distance. I knew there would be more of the same tomorrow and the days, weeks and months that lay ahead.

The next day did not yield the opportunity, I had hoped for, to make up for my thoughtlessness of the previous day. I did not remember that I had an early-morning flight to Hargeisa, the capital of the breakaway Republic of Somaliland.

When the Somali Republic collapsed in 1991 with the overthrow of the government of Siade Barre in the civil war, the former British Somaliland seceded. It became known as the Republic of Somaliland and maintained a level of peace and security that was totally lacking in its southern neighbor. No one, including the United Nations, recognized the new nation. It was felt that encouraging fragmentation was not the way to reconcile the warring factions. However, the government in the breakaway Republic was adamant to maintain its sovereignty and its relative peaceful existence, even in its isolation.

The calm was shattered, on occasions, by some clan violence, usually a spillover from the fighting in the south. There were also bands of lawless youths who had deserted the traditions of old. They showed no respect for their elders, and went their own way exacerbating the already chaotic situation.

My flight took off from the airport in Mogadishu and one hour and a half later we touched down in Hargeisa. A car was waiting for me, but there was a slight delay when a self-appointed customs officer insisted on checking my bags. I did not argue but allowed the young man to proceed while his two colleagues, armed with AK-47s, looked on. They must have thought that I had US dollars in my luggage, but they were mistaken. I knew that the government did not condone the unauthorized search, but it was powerless to stop things like that from happening. I endured the search and before long, was on my way to the office.

It only took a day to conclude my business, which included a review of project activities. I also met with a former staff member who had threatened violence against the Project Manager if his demand for adequate severance pay was not satisfied. The staff member was employed by the project for the past two years. His attendance at work was, at best, sporadic over the preceding six months. The Project Manager had been sympathetic even granting time to the staff member to attend the funerals of "three" maternal grandmothers. I had terminated the contract after reading the many letters the Project Manager had written to the staff member and his responses which were always apologetic with promises to do better. However, there was no improvement, so I made the decision to let him go.

I decided that since I had made the decision to fire the staff member, and had written him to that effect, I should deal with him and his threat against the Project Manager. After making sure the former staff member was not armed, he and I had a meeting. I told him in no uncertain terms that I was responsible for terminating his employment and that the office would not be blackmailed under any circumstance. He had said nothing except that he would meet with me again in Mogadishu. I had taken his remarks as a veiled threat, and knew that I had to be vigilant in the future.

The next day I was back at my usual routine in Mogadishu. The little boy I had met earlier was not in my thoughts as I walked home that day. But, there he was sitting in precisely the same place as before. That time I had stopped and said a few words to him that he did not understand. Just across the street was a cigarette vendor, Mahmud, whom I called over to translate for me. Before Mahmud reached us, I had lifted the child from the dirt road, and placed him on a low wall that ran the length of the road. As I lifted him, I noticed his paralyzed legs for the first time; legs that could not have borne his weight. The fact that he could not walk explained why he was crawling in the dirt road; and for sitting down with discarded trash around him.

Mahmud's questions went unanswered at first and only after some coaxing did he manage to elicit the name "Aden". Another surprise, Aden was not able to speak lucidly and, after some effort he was able to get the words out. His comprehension was good; it was just his speech impediment that got in the way. He did not know how old he was, but Mahmud estimated Aden's age to be about 10 years. He also found out that Aden lived, with his grandfather and other family members, in the same neighborhood, about half a mile from where we stood. Aden had crawled every day in the dusty road from his home to the place where I had first seen him. He had been doing that for months; however, our paths had crossed, by chance, just a few days before.

I thanked Mahmud, went to the gate of my residence, which was a few yards away, and called the caretaker, Kaleefah to come and assist me. I asked her to assure Aden that we had his best welfare in mind. He looked up trustingly as I bent, lifted him up and carried him into the residence. Without any instructions, Kaleefah carried Aden to the bathroom intending to strip him of his filthy clothes and give him a bath. She explained later that, though she did not have any clothing for him, she would have improvised until something suitable was found.

Kaleefah gasped as she removed Aden's clothing. I looked over her shoulder, and puzzlement must have shown on my face because both of us were looking at the genitalia of a female. Aden was not a boy, but a little girl. Both of us had assumed that Aden was a boy because of the short hair and clothing. It also did not occur to us that anyone would send a girl out in the streets to beg, particularly in her condition. Perhaps that was why she had short hair and clothes to give the illusion of being male.

We were so taken aback by our discovery that we were speechless and continued to stare until a low whimpering sound came from Aden. She was apparently frightened by our involuntary exclamations, not knowing why we were startled. Immediately, we became aware that she was looking at us, we both turned and left the room after assuring her that we would be back. Kaleefah had noticed a number of sores on Aden's behind and a few on her upper legs, so she called the United Nations doctor to come and attend to her. Kaleefah also sent for Mahmud and asked him to explain where Aden said she lived.

The doctor came and dressed Aden's sores. He suspected that she had parasites from all that time she had spent in the dirt, but wanted to get parental approval before he ran any tests. By the time the doctor had finished with Aden, Mahmud, who had gone to look for Aden's family, returned with an aunt. She told us that the family was concerned about Aden when she did not return home at her usual time. The aunt also told us that Aden had contracted polio when she was about four, and the disease had crippled her.

I had a lot of questions for the aunt, but did not want to cause her any embarrassment, by questioning her about the apparent ill treatment of a disabled child and a girl at that. The aunt was asked to take Aden to the United Nations Clinic the next day for treatment. The two of them were then driven home by one of my drivers.

Aden was not in her usual place the following day. She was also not there the next or the day after that. I had a feeling that it was no coincidence. I was worried, so I sent Kaleefah to Aden's home to find out what had happened to her. The grandfather took Aden's affliction as Allah's will and regarded any intervention on her behalf as interfering in things that were beyond our comprehension. According to the grandfather, the disease visited on Aden was what Allah had ordained for her.

I felt that something had been lost in the message, so I decided to visit Aden's grandfather to find out first-hand what made him tick. Aden was sitting outside the house, in the dirt, when I arrived. She gave me her brightest smile to date, no doubt happy to have seen me. I had spoken to her, although I knew she could not understand what I was saying. I felt, however, that she understood that I was concerned for her welfare. As I spoke to Aden, an old man came out of the house and identified himself as her grandfather. He assumed that I was the United Nations man who had taken such an interest in Aden..

Aden's grandfather was truly perplexed, and asked, several times, why I was so interested in his granddaughter. He told me it was Allah's will that Aden had been afflicted with polio and that no one should intervene in what Allah had ordained. I tried, as best I knew how, to explain my sense of compassion for Aden; that she touched me in a special way. I also spoke about my Christian outlook. I talked about Jesus' compassion for the sick, the lame and children. Even as I spoke, I tried to tread carefully to make sure that the grandfather understood I was not making any comparisons between his religion and mine. No contrasts were made between the philosophies of Islam and Christianity.

Before I left I asked the grandfather to allow Aden, accompanied by one of her aunts, to travel to Nairobi to see an orthopedic surgeon. I explained that perhaps she could be fitted with braces and provided with crutches so that she would not have to crawl around in the dirt anymore. Aden's grandfather reluctantly agreed to accept my offer. At that point I left, after saying that I had planned to be away on vacation for about three weeks. I also said that, my return, I hoped to have all the information for the family on the proposed trip to Nairobi. I also explained that the family would not be obligated to pay any of the expenses involved. It was important for the grandfather to understand that the family was free to contribute to Aden's treatment in any way they could, hence the statement about "obligation". I left after saying good-bye to Aden. There was no way I could have known that was the last time I would see her.

As promised, I returned to Mogadishu by the end of March 1993 and went to look for Aden. I had made arrangements at the Nairobi Hospital for her treatment and, at the same time, consulted with an orthopedic specialist who had agreed to take her case. I was looking forward to seeing Aden again, particularly with the good news about the arrangements for her travel to Nairobi. As soon as I reached the place I had last seen her, I felt something was not right. The house was empty; no one lived there anymore. The neighbors did not know where the family went. According to them, Aden's family had just packed up and moved.

I was saddened by the turn of events, not being able to fully appreciate why my offer to help the unfortunate girl had been rejected. I tried, through my contacts, to get information about Aden but to no avail. I looked for her until the day I left Somalia for good but never found out where she was, or what had happened to her. I concluded that, in the end, Aden's grandfather's belief took precedence over her welfare. He was convinced that her destiny was ordained by God, and therefore did not take God's compassionate attribute into account.

6

The Vulnerable

"She is still a prisoner of her childhood; attempting to create a new life, she reencounters the trauma."
Judith Lewis Herman

Monotony and boredom are reluctant companions born out of being in the same place on a constant basis. When people find themselves in situations like those, they often latch on things that bring them relief from the sameness of each passing day. There is also another type of monotony that involves culture. Monotony in this case refers to the sameness in the practice of mistreating females, generation after generation. This reference to generational monotony involves mutilating females that affect them even when they are complicit in perpetrating the culture. These two disparate conditions have the same effect in degrading the human spirit and, unfortunately, are repeated with disastrous results.

I believe that Jim, an American, the Water Project Manager became a victim of unrelenting boredom and sought ways to cope. While some people turn to alcohol to assuage their monotonous existence, Jim avoided it because of the effect it had on him. He knew that alcohol was a depressant, slowing body functions as the drinker goes into a euphoric state. The feeling of ecstasy is short-lived and could result in a hangover depending on the amount of alcohol that was consumed. Jim needed a substance that would facilitate a smoother transition from boredom to a feeling of well-being; something that had a more lasting effect, and that something was **qat**.

Instead of using alcohol as an escape, Jim turned to qat and became dependent on the amphetamine released by the drug after prolonged chewing. That was the high Jim sought. He did not wait for weekends to indulge in his favorite pastime, but kept a wad of qat between his upper jaw and his cheek all day long. The only time he parted company with his drug of choice was at mealtime. I assumed that he even slept with qat in his mouth without fear of swallowing it.

Chewing qat was the farthest thing from my mind; because I was afraid of the unknown effects it would have on my body. The same was true of Ganja (marijuana) that was available to me as a young man growing up in Belize. I never touched the stuff for the same reason that I stayed away from qat. Actually, that statement is not quite correct. I tried Ganja, once, when I was on assignment in Guyana.

A friend and I bought some Ganja and, after a few puffs, and yes, I did inhale, I became violently ill. So sick, in fact, that I thought I was going to die and was ready to write my will. I have no idea why the sudden onslaught of nausea and vomiting. Suffice it to say that was the first and last time I smoked Ganja, or took any type of recreational drug except alcohol.

I had, on many occasions, been with people as they chewed qat, waxed poetic or merely became mellow as the drug took its effect. No voices rose in anger or frustration, and no one became belligerent or wanted to fight. According to Somalis, the drug had the effect of calming frayed nerves and fostered tranquility. Those qualities of qat were the selling points by those who wanted others to try it out. Whenever someone asked me if I wanted to chew, I always begged off, and if I attended a qat session I carried my drug, usually "Tanqueray" gin.

One day Jim was going to a qat party and invited me to come along. He had done so many times before, but I did not accept the invitations mainly because the parties he attended were all night sessions, and I did not particularly relish going out after dark. I also had a recurring nightmare that I was stranded away from the residence, and was unable to return home, because of unrest in the city. When Jim asked me to go with him I thought about refusing, but finally decided to take a chance and attend the party. Perhaps my fear of not being able to get back to the safety of my residence was not justified.

We arrived at the party late in the evening. Jim did not tell me we were the only invitees. The house belonged to Amal, a young woman with whom Jim had struck up an intimate relationship. There were two other women, relatives of Amal, staying in the house. We assumed that the women must have been chewing qat before we arrived because by that time they were in a mellow, festive mood.

They were laughing and dancing to some shrill Arabic music. Their hands were painted with henna, subdued colors, but distinctive and quite noticeable. They were all dressed in typical Somali clothes, long skirts and blouses with long sleeves. Their heads were bare displaying long flowing hair, attractive women who knew that they were and were not shy in showing off their beauty. They were all dancing except for one of them: who sat demurely in a corner scarcely moving except for her eyes that took in everything in the room.

Jim introduced me to the women who knew a number of things about me. They knew that I was from Belize, and even knew where it was. As one of them said:

"Straddled between Mexico and Guatemala, official languages English and Spanish with beautiful beaches just like the beaches in Mogadishu."

I assumed that Jim had told them about me and Belize. I was wrong with regard to the latter. Jim had mentioned that I was from Belize, nothing more. Later in the night when I asked how they knew so much about Belize, Amal told me that education was not altogether unknown to Somalis and that they were quite capable of doing their own research. At that point, Amal took me to a part of the house where there were several bookshelves with rows upon rows of books, including a copy of the Encyclopedia Britannica.

The house was lit by candles and two or three kerosene lamps. There was a dining table in one corner of the living room that had platters of oranges, bananas, mangoes and papayas. The room was quite large with two spacious sitting areas. There were carpets tastefully arranged on the concrete floor. I do not remember any paintings on the walls that were recently painted in pale blue. There was a slight, but pleasant smell of incense that wafted throughout the house. I later found out that the smell came from burning myrrh.

Jim and I were offered wads of qat soon after we arrived at the party, but I refused and asked for a glass and some water. The women were not surprised by my refusal and my request for a glass. That reminded me that they knew more about me than I did about them. One of the women gave me a glass and placed a pitcher of water on the table. While they chewed qat, talked and danced I took several drinks and joined in the conversation, mainly about what was happening in Somalia and the world. I was ill at ease thinking about staying the night or driving back to the residence in the wee hours of the morning. I decided on the former, so I settled down and became engaged with my surroundings and the pleasant company of Jim and the women.

After a while I was drawn to the woman who sat alone observing, but not talking. I was sure that she must have been stunning during better times; dark complexioned, aquiline features with a slightly blunt nose. She had eyes that flashed with amusement when someone said something funny. It was obvious she was following each thread of the conversation although she was not participating. She knew that I had taken an interest in her, but she did not seem to care.

To tell the truth, I was not aware that I was staring at the woman, which was rude under any circumstance, until one of the other women came and sat beside me. Very quietly she asked why I had fixed my gaze on the woman across the room. She asked if I wanted to strike up a relationship with her cousin, who was a house guest and was passing through Mogadishu on her way to Baidoa, a town to the south of Mogadishu.

That was when I realized that I had, inadvertently, violated the protocol of good behavior. My interest centered on a vivid imagination of what this woman must have suffered in her life. It was obvious that she had seen hardships that may have been difficult for her to relate. She was almost as emaciated as some of the people, mostly women and children; I had seen in the refugee camps in Mogadishu. It was obvious also that she had missed many meals, and perhaps had escaped from one of the many refugee camps in the country.

I wondered if she was married and had children. If she were, where was her family? Her face was etched with so many untold misery that she may not have shared with her cousins. Women and children were more vulnerable than men, to the vagaries of marauding bands of thugs. Unless she was extremely lucky, rape and physical assaults were not outside the realm of possibilities. I wanted to ask her about the things that crossed my mind, but I felt I would have invaded her privacy. Perhaps by my asking I would have forced her to relive things she did not want to remember. The more I thought about her plight the more I was determined to engage her in conversation and perhaps some of her story would come out.

The suggestion that I was drawn to this woman, on a strictly physical level, was demeaning. It relegated me, in my mind, to the same strata as those men she had met on her journey; those men who, despite her circumstances, had seen her merely as a sex object and had taken advantage of her being female. I was insulted to say the least, and expressed my feelings, in a gentle matter-of-fact tone, to the woman who had questioned me. She apologized and was genuinely sorry for misreading my intentions. She too had been assaulted, and was scarred beyond my ability to understand what she went through, to truly appreciate the pain so many women, in that part of the world, endured.

Somehow, after her first assessment, she was drawn to me. She felt comfortable when she realized that my interest, in her cousin, was strictly from a humanitarian standpoint. She repeated her name to make sure that I would remember her apart from the others. The reason that was important to her escaped me until later when she related her story.

Her name was Halgan and, after serving me a dish of Somali rice, a blend of rice, vegetables, raisins and spices, topped with roasted lamb she gave me an insight into her life. The other women and Jim had joined us as she spoke, turning the party into a time of storytelling. Halgan spoke about her life growing up among a group of nomads, who lived in the desert in the northern part of the country. She, like most Somalis, who led pastoral lives, did not know the exact date of her birth. Important events, such as the birth of a child, were marked by some lunar or seasonal event. Days of the week, months and years took on less significance to the nomad than water, the seasons, the sun, rain, and storms.

She told us that she was born during a sand storm that killed almost half of the family's livestock. The storm ravaged the community the same year that Siad Barre became president of Somalia. Halgan was luckier than most because she knew that 1969 was the year in which she was born. She had no idea of the month or day, but that did not matter to her.

"Since I do not know my date of birth, I do not have to worry about celebrating birthdays," She said with some mirth in her voice.

She remembered being happy as a child chasing small animals in the desert, trying to keep up with zebras and foxes as she romped with her friends. The daily ritual of milking the camels and drinking the warm milk were pure joy. All that changed, when she was about five years old. She endured the horrendous and painful procedure of infibulation that would prepare her for marriage when she came of age. I did not know what infibulation meant, but assumed it had something to do with female circumcision. I refrained from asking for clarification, at the time, not wanting to interrupt the flow of the story.

Halgan was particularly angry with her mother and Somali women in general, for allowing the barbaric practice to continue. She knew that, even as she was speaking, countless girls were mutilated, and no one was there to champion their cause. She felt violated, not by a man, but by her mother who had held her down while an old gypsy woman performed the operation. She spoke, and we could feel her sorrow, being powerless to halt a practice rooted in culture. That culture perpetuated the myth that women came into the world with something evil between their legs. That horrible thing made them dirty, oversexed and not suitable for marriage until it was excised.

Halgan knew that she had to get away from Somalia for herself and daughters that she hoped to have in the future. She decided that no child of hers would go through the degrading and painful process of infibulation. She had relatives in England, the Netherlands and the USA, and had already started the process of trying to immigrate. She knew that unless she met a Somali man with a progressive outlook, her husband would have to be a foreigner. She also envisaged a life outside Somali communities no matter where they were. She had heard that the practice of infibulation was not only relegated to Africa and Arabia, but was also performed in the West where those cultures had taken root.

The reflection on female circumcision caused the mood of the party to change from gaiety to somber contemplation. The women cried softly. I thought that they were all thinking about their own experiences, and perhaps how they could escape as Halgan had decided she would do. As she spoke I began to admire her strength and resolve. My hope was that my daughters, who were a few years younger than Halgan, would develop her qualities, her strength and fortitude as they made their way in this cruel and sometimes unrelenting world.

Morning came, and we were still talking. It was Friday, the Muslim holy day, so we decided to stay for the rest of the day, not to indulge in such deep conversation, but just to relax. We went to a neighborhood market and purchased fruits, vegetables and goat meat. When we returned, the women cooked while Jim chewed qat, and I drank some more gin as we waited for the meal that was being prepared. The women made samosas, a delectable version of the Indian pastry with the same name, curried chick peas, and a spongy, fermented pancake called anjero. The meal was much better than those served at the residence and, for a few minutes, I toyed with the idea of asking Amal and Halgan to take over the kitchen. However, I did not broach the subject with them except to comment on their excellent culinary skills.

Before leaving Amal's home, I asked her how she could feel safe in a house occupied by women without any male protection. I recalled Khadija's story and was truly perplexed at Amal's apparent lack of concern for her safety. She smiled and thanked me for my obvious fear for her safety. She took me across the street and introduced me to a young man, her cousin. He did not smile, just nodded his head acknowledging the introduction. As we were walking back to Amal's house, I commented on the young man's deportment. She said that he was always like that from the time he was a child. This was where she grew up surrounded by relatives, so she felt quite safe. We returned to the residence before nightfall much the wiser for what I had learned in the past twenty-four hours.

I could not contain my curiosity about infibulation. Those days were well before the Google age; therefore I had to find a book on the subject or ask someone about it. A few days after hearing Halgan's story, I spoke with a woman named Zarah about infibulation. She was a professor at the university before the civil war and belonged to a group of women who banded together, across clan lines, to take care of orphaned children, casualties of the war. I had turned to Zarah for help in finding Aden when she and her family had disappeared, but she too had failed to find out anything about the family.

I had been to Zarah's home on several occasions with some colleagues to discuss her project with children, and arrange financial support for them to carry on with their good work. Zarah also ran a school in our residence that had about a dozen children, ranging from seven to ten years old. Some UNDP colleagues and I paid the teachers' salaries and bought books, blackboard, chalk, paper and pencils for the school.

When I brought up the subject of infibulation, Zarah was somewhat embarrassed, not because the subject was taboo in Somali circles. She felt awful because she was also, like so many other women, ashamed that the practice was still quite prevalent in the country. She believed that the procedure was invasive and barbaric and expressed her concern that infibulation was still practiced under unsanitary, conditions among nomadic clans.

Zarah would not discuss the subject further because it was too painful for her. Instead, she gave me a magazine that had an article on infibulation that I was to return to her when I was finished. It only took reading the first few paragraphs of the article to understand why the women felt such pain, and found the practice so difficult to discuss. The pain was one thing, the feeling of degradation was worse.

The procedure entailed the removal of the labia minora and the inner surfaces of the labia majora. The remaining tissue is sewn together leaving only a small hole for the passage of urine and menstrual blood. After the procedure, the legs are tied together from the ankles to the hips causing any movement next to impossible. Making the patient immobile was intended to assist in the healing process. The patient is left in solitude away from the village for about two weeks while her every need is attended to by her mother or other close female relatives. Many children die from infection when the procedure is performed under unsanitary conditions.

The description of the procedure was so vivid that I felt sick to the pit of my stomach. I wondered how any mother, after having endured the pain and suffering of infibulation, could allow her daughter to be butchered with their assistance. I did not understand the culture and, therefore, felt only anger against people who perpetrated such abuse.

I did not go back to Amal's home because there was renewed inter-clan fighting. However, I saw her and Halgan many times when they came to the residence to visit Jim and me, usually for dinner or lunch on Fridays.

I understood why Jim was fond of Amal during those visits. I came to know her quite well with her winning smile, her intelligence and outgoing personality. She could be the life of the party but, at the same time, was capable of discussing complex issues, like the role of the United Nations in Somalia, and her thoughts on why the mission was bound to fail. Halgan was also an exemplary young woman, strong willed and confident in her ability to change her life.

Sometime in April 1993 Jim decided that he would not renew his contract with the Water Project, which was due for renewal at the end of that month. His decision followed several months of neglecting his duties, which resulted in loss in production. Qat had taken over. As such, nothing was as important to Jim as getting high and maintaining the mood. The problem of his inattention to details came to a head one day when, because of his negligence, the project ran out of diesel for the generators at the pumping stations.

It took almost five days for the delivery of diesel to be made. During that period, about half the city was out of water and, about a week after that incident, Jim relocated to Nairobi. Before he left, I had a long talk with him. I told him about my concern for his welfare, and that I saw he was in a downward spiral of addiction. I wanted to help, or at least to let him know that I was there for him. He had assured me he knew what he was doing and that he would be just fine. Neither he nor I believed what he said, but I could do nothing except to tell him that if he needed help he should contact me.

Several weeks later, when I was in Nairobi, I found out where Jim lived and went to see him. On a certain level, I was sorry that I did. He was living with a local woman in squalid conditions. The shack in which they lived was about 100 square feet with mud walls, dirt floor and corrugated tin roof. There was no running water, and the communal toilet, a few feet from his shack, was a hole in the ground surrounded by corrugated metal sheets.

I knew he had quite a sum of money, at least $10,000 and asked him how he could feel safe in the community. He assured me that no one, including his woman, knew that he was a "thousandiare". He had his stash strapped to his leg near the groin. Life was cheap in Nairobi. Jim could be injured, or lose his life for less princely sums, but he was confident that he could take care of himself. Before I left, Jim went inside his shack, then walked with me down the hill to the place where my transport was waiting. He got into the vehicle with me and slipped something in my pocket at the same time saying in a whisper "that is for Amal".

On my return to Mogadishu, I sent a message to Amal that I wanted to see her. A few days later Amal and Halgan came to the residence. Both women were dressed from head to toe in pale green attire and shawls. Amal's face was covered; only her eyes were visible. I had invited them inside, but they said they were on their way to the doctor. Amal had contracted hepatitis and was being treated for the disease. I offered the services of the UN doctor, but Amal was confident that she was receiving good treatment. I gave her the money; $2000 Jim had slipped into my pocket. She thanked me and left saying that they would see me soon.

That was the last time I saw either of them. About a week later, I got word from Halgan that Amal was dead. She went to bed one night, and the following morning her lifeless body was found by a relative. Since an autopsy was not performed, the actual cause of death could not be determined with any degree of certainty. The doctor assumed that her death was caused by complications from hepatitis. I felt a profound sadness on hearing about Amal's death. I berated myself for not insisting that she consulted the UN doctor. Perhaps she would have lived under his care. I realized that it was useless to try to recreate the past. Thinking about what should have been done would not change what had happened.

Halgan had also told me that she was preparing to leave Somalia for Holland. She had relatives there and hoped she would be granted political asylum in Holland or the USA. About a week after receiving her messages, I went to her home to give her my address in the USA, in case she decided to make the USA her home. However, she had already left Mogadishu, and I did not hear from her again.

Sometime in mid-May 1993 I went back to the Nairobi address I had for Jim. I wanted to inform him about Amal's death and to see how he was doing, but he was not there. Someone living near the shack Jim had occupied told me that the "white man" and his wife had moved to Mombasa.

I had tasked several people who went to Mombasa, who knew Jim, to try to locate him. It should not have been too difficult to get information on a white American living with a black woman in Mombasa, but no one found out anything about him. It was as if he had disappeared from the face of the earth, or maybe he did not want to be found. I guess I will never know.

In the meantime, the situation in Mogadishu and the southern part of the country was sliding, inexorably, into anarchy as it was before the advent of UNITAF. General Aidid became more aggressive in his attacks on UNOSOM II's policies. He used his radio station to spread rumors about the U.N.'s intentions in Somalia. Disarmament, that was an integral part of the March 1992 agreement, was being portrayed as an attempt to colonize Somalia once more.

Aidid refused to take part in any discussions that promoted the establishment of a functioning government, unless he took the lead role. He felt that Somalis should be left alone to solve Somalia's problems. Foreign inputs were not appreciated no matter how well-intentioned. However his insistence that foreign inputs, particularly those from UNOSOM II, were a hindrance, did not include funds he needed to hold meetings. He expected the United Nations and other foreign entities to fund his political activities, under the guise that those activities were means he employed to bring about reconciliation of the warring factions.

At the end of May 1993, Aidid called a Peace Conference in Mogadishu and invited the various factions to attend. True to his assertions that foreign entities were not needed, UNOSOM II was not consulted on any matter relating to the conference, or invited to be present. However, after the meeting, Aidid submitted a detailed account of the expenditure his organization incurred with a demand for reimbursement. Since UNOSOM II did not sanctioned the conference, it refused to pay. Three days after Aidid's conference, UNOSOM II also organized another Peace Conference in Kismayo, a city to the south of Mogadishu.

Ali Mahdi and groups allied to him were invited to attend the meeting, but Aidid's representative was excluded. Aidid regarded UNOSOM II's actions as a deliberate attempt to isolate him. He also saw it as a hostile act. With that, and other perceived slights, the stage was set for the outbreak of hostilities between UNOSOM II and Aidid's militia.

7

In the Wrong Place

"Arrogance diminishes wisdom"
Arabian Proverb

Before the May 1993 peace conference in Kismayo that added to the schism between Aidid and Ali Mahdi, UNOSOM had sponsored two peace conferences in Addis Ababa, Ethiopia in January and March 1993. Both initiatives were unsuccessful since UNOSOM, American and European contributors did not understand or respect the Somali way of making peace called "shir". Several people, who had expert knowledge of the country and its people warned that the Organizations, involved in trying to bring Somalia back into the community of nations, were trying to push through neatly conceived solutions too quickly. Their warnings went unheeded with disastrous results.

Bureaucrats at UN Headquarters in New York also did not want to waste their valuable time on a bunch of nomads, reclining under trees and conferring for months on their divergent views. The Somalis, on the other hand, did not understand what the rush was about. They did not feel that they had accomplished anything at the conferences and just signed documents that were placed before them. Shortly after the March conference one participant remarked:

"The speeches were nice, the slogans were good, but the whole thing was quite meaningless."

UNOSOM had failed to convince Aidid and his allies that they should work together for the good of their country. As a result, the security situation deteriorated into hostilities between the Peacekeepers and Aidid's militia. The two groups clashed on several occasions with few casualties. However, the fighting was disconcerting to the International Community, because conflict disrupted the work they had painstakingly built up over the past five months.

Shortly after the Kismayo Peace Conference, to which Aidid's representative was not invited, the pro Ali Mahdi radio station announced that the groups, allied to him, were in complete accord with the United Nations plans for Somalia. The intended consequence of the broadcasts was to incite resistance on Aidid's part, especially when the broadcasts insinuated that there was an agreement to hand over all assets to UNOSOM II. Assets included mass media equipment, information centers, pamphlets, vehicles and anything that contributed to instability in the country. Arms and ammunition were on the top of the list of things that fueled the fires of unrest. Ali Mahdi also implicated UNOSOM II in an alleged plan to reconstitute the Somali Republic with little, if any, contribution from Somali leaders.

UNOSOM II had never endorsed the assertions of Ali Mahdi and his allies. The discussions always centered on reconciliation of the factions, establishment of a national police force and reconstituting the judicial system. All those things and more were necessary before the state would emerge. That day was a long way off, but Aidid viewed Ali Mahdi's rhetoric and his blatant support for UNOSOM II as threats to his survival.

In retrospect, it was understandable that Aidid became suspicious when UNOSOM II informed him of plans to inspect his radio station on June 5. He believed the intent was to seize his radio station and the ammunition depot, neither of which was acceptable to him. He had no intentions of handing over his assets to UNOSOM II because his enemy, Ali Mahdi, said he should. Therefore, while UNOSOM II was making plans to carry out the inspection, which was in reality just that--an inspection, Aidid was making plans of his own.

In the predawn hours of Saturday June 5 1993, a platoon of Pakistani soldiers moved out of their compound and drove through the streets of Mogadishu. Twenty-four of those brave men had no idea that June 5 was their last day in this life. They did not know that, before the day was over, they would come face to face with their Maker in accordance with their staunch belief in The Prophet's teachings.

The briefing, on the evening before the mission, was cursory. The Commanding Officer informed the platoon that their mission was straightforward. It was being carried out in accordance with an agreement between the warring factions; that periodic checks would be made by UNOSOM II on the quantity of arms each group held in their arsenal.

Aidid's radio station was strategically located on high ground near the center of Mogadishu, close to the Green Line that separated the forces of Aidid from those of Ali Mahdi. At least two weeks before UNOSOM II informed Aidid about the inspection, the radio station had been inciting his followers to rebel against UNOSOM II. The broadcasts informed listeners that the real reason for the inspection was to destroy the radio station and seize the arms and ammunition. Aidid's followers believed the message, and as the Pakistani soldiers reached their destination Aidid's followers ambushed them, killing twenty-four and injuring forty-four in the ensuing battle. Aidid's followers' sustained casualties also including twenty-five killed and 100 injured.

The U.N. Security Council convened the following day, June 6 and adopted Resolution 837. It gave UNOSOM II the authority to use a more aggressive military stance against Aidid since he was culpable in the attack on the Pakistanis. Within the next few days, Pakistani and Italian forces conducted several armored patrols throughout the city but concentrated in the area where the ambush took place. The strength of those patrols kept Aidid's militia at bay

General Hoar, the commanding officer of the US forces, petitioned Washington and received four Air Force AC-130 gunships and specially modified C-130 cargo planes to support direct ground assaults against Aidid's militia. The planes took part in thirty missions over Mogadishu, eight of which were combat sorties.

Raids over Mogadishu on June 11 and 12 demolished two of Aidid's weapons storage facilities and destroyed the radio station's transmission capacity. During the days that followed, the American military destroyed other weapons storage sites and vehicle compounds belonging to Aidid and his key supporters. The actions by the Americans, and other coalition forces served to harden Aidid's resolve to resist with the result that skirmishes, between, the two opposing forces increased in intensity. On June 17, Admiral Howe issued a warrant for Aidid's arrest and authorized $25,000 reward leading to his capture.

On July 3, the Italians conducted a house to house search near the border between the north and south sections of Mogadishu. They were withdrawing from the area when women and children erected barricades of twisted steel and burning tires. They stoned the Italians while snipers opened fire killing three Italians and wounding 20 others.

On July 12, a number of American Black Hawk and Little Bird helicopters fired TOW missiles on Abdi House, a compound where, according to intelligence reports, a meeting of Aidid and some of his lieutenants was in progress. There was no warning that a raid was imminent. As a result, the attack caught the occupants of the building by surprise as they were preparing to discuss the dire situation in the country.

The intelligence provided to the Americans was wrong. Aidid was neither at the meeting nor was he expected to attend. I found out later that influential elders and leaders of Aidid's sub-clan, the Habar Gidir, had met several times, before the Abdi House meeting, to discuss Aidid's continued belligerence against UNOSOM II and the resultant tensions that existed in the country.

There were some hardliners at the meeting at Abdi House; men who wanted control of the country in their hands regardless of the suffering that was being inflicted on the Somali people. A number of moderates were also present to argue their case against antagonizing UNOSOM II. Both the moderates and the hardliners knew the power of the US military. Unlike the hardliners, the moderates felt that they could not win if the Americans unleashed the full power of their military against them. The moderates, mostly businessmen, made efforts to stop inter clan violence that affected commerce and their ability to accumulate wealth.

In their slow and deliberate process both groups were trying to decide, among themselves, what was to be done with the main cause of the problem, General Aidid. Their efforts to rein in the recalcitrant warlord brought disaster on them. The result was a catastrophe not only for the unfortunate people who were in the compound at the time of the attack, but also for innocent people who died in retaliation for the strike by the Americans.

The meeting with about 90 men in attendance had scarcely begun when the first TOW missile hit the building. Many influential men died, including the clan's most senior leader, ninety year old Sheik Haji Mohamed Iman Aden. One survivor reported that he saw a flash of light followed by a violent crack. The blast from the first explosion knocked him to the floor, and as he stood up and took one step forward he heard the whoosh of a second missile, then another powerful explosion. The blast threw him to the floor again as thick smoke filled the room. He tried to move forward but bodies, a bloody pile of men and parts of men blocked his path. He could not recall how he escaped but remembered running away from the carnage and the building that was engulfed in flames.

Sixty-nine prominent members of Aidid's sub-clan died that day. We will never know what the outcome of the meeting would have been if the deliberations had not ended prematurely by the attack. On the other hand I found out, almost immediately after the attack, that UNOSOM II and the Americans had turned some of the moderates in Aidid's camp against any attempts at a peaceful solution to the conflict.

The news of the tragedy spread like wildfire throughout the city. The wailing and sorrow in its aftermath transcended clan lines and cries for justice could be heard in every corner of Mogadishu. Mobs roamed the streets setting fire to tires with the black, putrid smell of burning rubber rising like incense on that bright and cloudless day. The mood of the crowds, chanting anti-UNOSOM slogans and demanding the death of Admiral Howe was an omen of things to come. Everyone in the International Community was warned to stay off the streets and not to engage Somalis in any dialogue.

Journalists were not immune from attack that day. Despite the warning to stay off the streets, five of them went to the scene of the attack, accompanied by Somalis who wanted the journalists to report to the world the atrocities committed by the Americans. The mob at the scene turned on the journalists killing four of them, two Kenyans, an American and a German. A Good Samaritan, who risked his life, rescued the fifth journalist by driving him away from the scene and took him to the El-Sahafi hotel where most foreigners were staying.

Soon after the June 5 massacre of the Pakistanis and the warrant was issued to apprehend Aidid, it became obvious that capturing him was not going to be an easy task. Intelligence reports showed that Aidid and his top aides had gone underground in the Black Sea area of Mogadishu, a slum with narrow streets and winding alleyways.

Admiral Howe concluded that the Peacekeepers did not have the capacity to launch attacks on Aidid's militia and decided to request Washington to deploy the elite Task Force Rangers. He had direct access to senior government officials in Washington, and used his contacts to try and convince them that he needed expert assistance to capture Aidid.

Between July and August, UNOSOM II lost ten Peacekeepers during skirmishes with Aidid's militia and resulted in Admiral Howe keeping up the pressure on Washington for the deployment of the crack US Rangers. In the first week of August, Aidid's militia detonated a remote-controlled landmine killing four American soldiers, and two weeks later another landmine injured seven others. After those attacks, President Clinton approved the deployment of the Rangers.

No one, except Howe and top military aides, knew that Task Force Rangers had arrived in Somalia on August 22 under the command of Major General William F Garrison. Their sole mission was to capture Aidid and his key lieutenants and hand them over to UNOSOM II. The job would prove particularly challenging because Aidid had gone underground after the attack on Abdi House and the raids on his strongholds in June and July.

Even before the Rangers arrived in Mogadishu, the CIA and military commanders in Mogadishu were making plans to capture Aidid and his advisers. The CIA had recruited many Somalis as paid informants (assets) some years earlier. One of their assets was a minor warlord from north Mogadishu. He had worked with the Agency before the US government had pulled out of Somalia during the height of the Civil War. Soon after CIA officers returned to Mogadishu in December 1992, they re-established contact with the warlord. Although his militia was fairly small, some 400 men, he had connections that were valuable to the CIA.

The warlord knew the streets of Mogadishu very well and had a working relationship with Aidid and a few of his advisers. He was therefore considered a valuable asset and was given a handler who had worked with him before.

The CIA devised a plan to plant a tracking device in an ivory-handled walking stick. The warlord would give the walking stick to Aidid as a token of friendship, a practice that was common in Somali culture. After that, tracking Aidid would have been a simple matter of following the beacon's signals. Everything was in place to capture the main source, according to Howe, of Somalia's problems. The plan was brilliant and once the device was planted a test was carried out to ensure that it was working as planned.

A few days after planting the device in the walking stick, a CIA officer tested its efficacy by traveling around Mogadishu with it for several hours. He went as far away as some thirty miles from the general location of the tracking tool. The Officer did not divulge, beforehand, where he intended to go, and likewise he was not told if the tracking tool was to be turned on for the entire test period or exactly where it was located. Only a few people knew about the test, as a matter of fact, only five Officers knew about the plan.

Conducting the test was almost as important as the plan to deliver the walking stick to Aidid. The test showed an electronics glitch in the tracking device with the result that the beacon did not give off any signals. The devices was repaired and tested again. The second test went off flawlessly and arrangements were made to deliver the walking stick.

However, since protocol had to be observed in making contact, the warlord took several days to approach his target. Aidid was a very cautious man, and no one had easy access to him, even those he knew and were considered allies. Messages were dispatched, by the warlord, to Aidid intimating that too much time had elapsed since the last meeting between friends and allies. Aidid agreed to meet around August 20, but it could have been conducted a day sooner or a day later. The warlord was also to be ready to meet within an hour's notice, at which time the venue would have been set.

In addition to the perils posed by living in a war torn country, men also played dangerous games to wile the time away when they were not engaged in killing each other. The night before the meeting with Aidid was to have taken place the warlord shot himself in the head while playing Russian roulette and died on the spot. The homing beacon was Plan A, but was foiled when the key element in the strategy gambled with his life and lost. Plan B had to be invoked which entailed physically looking for and apprehending Aidid. That was to be the job of the US Rangers.

8

U.S. Rangers Assault U.N. Employees

"To himself everyone is immortal;
He may know that he is going to die,
But he can never know that he is dead"
Samuel Butler

Explosion after explosion rocked the building and it quickly filled with smoke; a gray mist with the strong smell of cordite and something else that was not easily discernible. It had seemed like an eternity before I was able to identify the smell, but it could only have been a few seconds as the speed of sound and smell escalated. Then, it occurred to me that the unidentified smell was fear; the fear that comes from being trapped, being vulnerable to something that was dangerous but not knowing exactly what that something was. It appeared to me that I was, within a few minutes, on my way to meet my Maker. I felt that I was going to die, but I also knew that I would not know when I was dead.

I did not think to pray, although I knew that prayer was needed to invoke some kind of divine intervention. It seemed pointless to appeal to God, to ask for His protection only in the face of danger and danger was the reality; fight, flight, or prayer. All three seemed futile exercises at that critical moment. As my fear increased in intensity and my heart beating at an unsustainable rate, the clock in my mind started to backtrack to the time and the reason why I was in that place at that time.

After Aidid's followers massacred the twenty-four Pakistani soldiers on June 5, there was a shift, for the worse, in the relationship between the Peacekeepers and Aidid's militia. The distrust between those entities turned into outright hostilities. It was unsafe, for United Nations staff to be on the streets of Mogadishu during the day, let alone at night so our offices and residences became our prisons. Up to that point, UN staff was not targeted by Aidid's militia. However, given Aidid's hatred of UNOSOM II, no one could predict what Aidid would do in the future.

With that in mind, Admiral Howe ordered a general evacuation of non-essential staff from Mogadishu to Nairobi. The evacuation would remain in effect until suitable accommodation was found adjacent to the airport that was considered a "safe" zone. The area was under extensive renovations because of damages that were sustained during the civil war. In the meantime, essential staff was relocated to the old US Embassy compound that was adjacent to the military camp. Other International Agencies and NGOs also relocated their offices and staff to Nairobi. Some remained in Mogadishu and were also accommodated in the old Embassy Compound. The cooperation among the UN offices and Aid Agencies was phenomenal.

UN staff, who relocated to the old Embassy compound, was housed in shipping containers converted to offices and sleeping quarters. As can be imagined, working, and living in such cramped lodgings added to the tension that already existed. No one felt safe because it would have been fairly easy for Aidid's militia to attack the compound with rocket propelled grenades if he were so inclined.

They could also have infiltrated the compound by climbing over the walls at vulnerable spots.

Everyone, military and civilian alike, ate in the mess hall. The food was not appetizing with practically the same menu for days on end. After a very short while, most people had dry goods brought in from Nairobi to supplement the food in the mess hall. It was truly a drab existence and staff got away, as often as was possible, to Nairobi or Mombasa.

I was away in New York on Home Leave and was on a flight to Nairobi on June 5 as the events were unfolding in Mogadishu. I had just cleared customs in Nairobi when I received news about the tragedy. The driver who came to pick me up from the airport handed me a long cable that described in detail what had occurred. I was also told to remain in

Nairobi and await further instructions. Later that same day I was asked to re-establish a satellite office in Nairobi.

It was also important to locate suitable buildings in the safe zone in Mogadishu for the planned return to the city once some measure of stability had returned. Although I would have preferred the comfort and relative safety of Nairobi, duty called, so I went to Mogadishu on June 20 with some measure of trepidation. The news on CNN and the local television station about the continued violence in Mogadishu, and other parts of the country did not help to allay my fears.

On that occasion, everyone on the flight had to wait at the Mogadishu airport for some two hours before we were allowed to travel to UNOSOM II compound. There were several hotspots in the city with inter-clan fighting and threats against the Peacekeepers. The day before our arrival thousands of Somalis had taken to the streets to demonstrate against alleged indiscriminate killing of Somalis. The day following my arrival did not bring any relief in the threat of attacks. I could not venture out of the compound to do the job I had gone to Mogadishu to do. Three days later I was still holed up in the compound, so I return to Nairobi.

On July 12, I made another trip to Mogadishu. The need to relocate staff to the "safe zone" had become even more critical since relief efforts were hampered by the absence of vital staff. That time I had to sleep at the airport because the whole city was in an uproar. Bands of Somalis roamed the streets and engaged the Peacekeepers in ongoing skirmishes. That was the day of the Abdi House incident when 69 Somali men were killed.

We went to UNOSOM II compound early the next morning under armed escort. We were on pins and needles as we were driven through the streets of Mogadishu. People were on the streets apparently waiting for something to spark another outburst of violence. They kept a respectful distance from the convoy because the escorts were heavily armed. In fact, everyone was pleased to see so many people on the roads because that meant no roadside bombs had been planted.

We arrived at the compound without incident and were glad to be in a "safe" place. That time it took two days before I could leave the compound, accompanied by a military escort, to inspect two buildings near the airport. The buildings were next to others that had already been rented by UNOSOM II and were being readied for staff. One of the buildings I saw would have been ideal except that it was completely gutted. All the pipes, toilets, sinks and kitchen equipment had been stolen.

The other building was not as large but required less renovation. I settled on that one and arranged to meet the owner to negotiate a lease. However, it took two days before we could meet. The situation had turned volatile in the streets again, and even law-abiding Somalis stayed indoors. We finally met at the airport on my way back to

Nairobi, shook hands on a gentleman's agreement with plans to sign the lease agreement within two weeks. In the meantime, the owner would proceed with the necessary renovation.

True to my word, I was back in Mogadishu two weeks later, but that time I decided to stay at the UNDP Water Project compound instead of UNOSOM II. I felt that I would be able to move about at will and be confined to the UN compound. I had informed the Chief of UN Security where I was staying in Mogadishu and the places I intended to visit while I was there. Everything went as planned and two days later I was back in Nairobi.

Aidid's militia was not the only entity that made Mogadishu such a dangerous place. Most people working to provide relief for famine victims; and helping to re-establish civil authority in a war torn country were also concerned with the dangers posed by American military helicopters. In actual fact, I was more afraid of "friendly fire" than of Aidid's militia, and was particularly worried about military activities in which helicopters were involved.

There were two occasions when rockets fired from helicopters struck buildings that were not targeted. In one incident, a building housing an NGO was hit by mistake and two Somalis were injured. The building was adjacent to the Water Project office building which was also damaged in the attack. All the window panes were shattered from the explosion next door. Mercifully no one was in the office at the time of the attack. The next day I inspected the building, and saw glass littering the floor of the office I had used on occasions. Two shards of glass had been driven through the back of my chair. If I had been at my desk that day, I would certainly have been injured or killed.

On the other occasion, a rocket damaged a UNOSOM II residence located some two miles (as the crow flies) from the scene of the military operation. Fortunately, the building was vacant. It was being readied for personnel who were scheduled to return to Mogadishu the next day. It took several weeks to repair the building and many more for staff to feel comfortable enough to move in.

Mogadishu was a dangerous place, and we were all concerned with humanitarian projects working in tandem with military operations. It was inevitable that these two activities, whether by accident or by design, would clash. It was only a matter of time before tragedy would strike.

I went back to Mogadishu on August 15 and was joined a few days later by Nawal Surial, an Administrative Officer. She had brought in US dollars to pay salaries and to have funds on hand to finalize renovations of the building we had leased. The Deputy Representative, Larry Du Bois, arrived on August 27, accompanied by a newly appointed United Nations Volunteer, Maurice O'Donnel. We stayed at the Water Project residence and conducted business from the office next door and also at the UNOSOM II compound. On August 29, we worked until about 2000 hours and retired to the residence for dinner. We worked in the residence until much later in preparation for a visit I had planned to Hargeisa for the next day.

After dinner, we decided to put on a movie. We looked through our sparse collection of video tapes and eventually settled on "Platoon." Unfortunately, it was in Italian without English sub titles. Since none of us spoke Italian, we decided on another film "Sleeping with the Enemy." We did not, of course, realize how much on track we were and that within a few hours we would be embroiled in an incident that could have ended tragically.

Before the first explosion was heard and felt, the drone of helicopters became a concern for me. The noise was deafening and continued for at least fifteen minutes before I realized that something was wrong. I checked my watch that was on my night stand, and noticed that it was 0300 hrs. The sound of helicopters flying overhead, as the Americans kept a close eye over Mogadishu, was not unusual. They were constantly on surveillance missions trying to locate and capture General Aidid. But that time something was different. Instead of hearing the sound of helicopters approaching my location, reaching a crescendo as they flew overhead and then diminishing as they flew away, the drone kept up its intensity, and the sound of the spinning rotors seemed to increase with every beat.

My heart was pounding ever so slightly, as I got up from my bed and peered through a nearby window to see what was going on. I could not see anything from my window, but something was definitely amiss. It occurred to me that there must have been a military operation in full progress somewhere in the neighborhood. I would have returned to bed at that time except that something was nagging at me to find out what was going on. I went next door to Larry's room and in the dim light saw him standing at his window looking out on the courtyard below.

"What in hell is going on Larry?" I asked as I approached the spot where he was standing.

He did not respond; instead he pointed at a helicopter that was hovering some 50 yards from where we stood. We could make out shadowy figures moving towards our residence in the semi dark. Instinctively we both knew that we were in danger, but we stood transfixed at the window, not knowing what our next move should be.

That was when I heard the first explosion, and I was brought back to the present suffocating in the smoke filled room, heavily infused with the smell of cordite. The vibration caused by the explosion was so great that the glass windows shattered. Shards and splinters of glass fell to the floor, some splinters showering us as we intuitively covered our eyes and moved away from the window. We retreated to the corridor between the bedrooms where we ran into

Nawal, one of the other occupants of the house. She was as frightened and confused as we were, coughing and trying to rub the sting of the smoke from our eyes.

The fourth occupant of the house, Maurice O'Donnell, was nowhere to be seen. He was forgotten in the confusion; no thought of him or thoughts to inquire what had happened to him. Larry, Nawal and I were focused on what was going on around us, trying to figure out why we were under attack.

The house was in complete darkness except for flashes of light from successive explosions as we stood in the corridor, totally confused and disoriented by the noise. Choking on smoke, our anxiety heightened as we heard shouts coming from downstairs. We were suddenly aware that a number of soldiers had ascended the stairs from below, and some had descended by way of a stairway leading from the roof.

It was not that we were aware of soldiers ascending and descending the stairways immediately. At first all we saw were figures with beams of light emanating from what appeared to be their heads and antennas protruding from different parts of their bodies. It also seemed that they had on masks emulating figures from outer space who were not accustomed to the earth's atmosphere.

As we stood there mesmerized by what was going on and what we were seeing, I realized that the figures that had invaded our space were soldiers. Their expletives and shouts in English commanding that we keep absolutely still and not to utter a word confirmed my deduction. I was slammed up against the wall as hands groped over by body, ostensibly checking for weapons. I was then pushed to the glass strewn floor all the while being assaulted with blows and kicks, and hearing the most abusive language I had ever heard in my life. I assumed that my colleagues were suffering the same fate.

I kept telling myself that all this was a terrible mistake and that, at some point, the people involved would come to their senses and stop the madness. But that was wishful thinking, they did not stop but continued their assault and the destruction of the building and our property. The attack actually increased in intensity as the tension in the room escalated; tension from fear coming from those being assaulted and tension from anger by those perpetrating the assault. Above the noise, the smoke, the curses using the "f" word in every utterance, the feelings that drove the soldiers were clear:

"We are "f" angry, very "f" angry!"

They did not say what they were angry about; they just kept repeating the words like a refrain giving impetus to continue with their assault. The words about being angry were supplemented with the command to be quiet and not to say a word. I could not tell if my colleagues were trying to speak, to explain who we were, even though we were close to each other.

I became aware that not a sound could be heard; the place had become as quiet as a tomb. That was most disconcerting, after being accustomed to the sound of explosions. At that point, I raised my head to look around. My movement was met with a boot on my back and the injunction from one of the soldiers:

"Do not move an "f" inch!"

We were then taken to the lower floor, together with Maurice who had been rounded up by that time. There was another figure, one of our guards, also bound and gagged lying on the floor. At first I thought he was dead, since I could not detect the slightest movement from him. He later told me that, although he could not understand what the soldiers were saying, he understood their gestures to mean that he was not to make a sound.

Before the soldiers took us to the lower floor, I spoke to one of the soldiers I had identified as the leader of the group. I told him who we were and that our identities could be confirmed from our documents that were in our rooms. He had gathered our national and UN passports and UNOSOM identity cards. He had radioed someone, presumably his superior officer, and gave the information contained in the various documents. The response he received was obvious as he turned to his colleagues and told them:

"We are going to take the two black guys, and leave the others."

He meant that they were going to take me and the chief security guard because everyone else was white. However Larry spoke up immediately and said:

"If anyone is being taken, then you must take all of us."

The platoon leader consulted with someone on his radio again. We knew what the answer was when we were marched out of the building with our trousers dangling around our legs. Only Nawal was left behind. Absolutely no consideration was given to her safety, being left in a building with absolutely no protection and every door blown off their hinges. We all thought that Nawal was also being taken, and were surprised that she was not with the group when we got outside. The platoon leader ignored both Larry and I when we protested that Nawal should not be left alone. As soon as we left the building we saw the six other guards, who were on duty that night, handcuffed and sitting on the ground.

The ten of us were marched at a quick trot about 100 yards up the road to another compound. By the dim moon light I could make out the expanse of the compound. It seemed to be quite big, but no structures were discernible. All of us were made to kneel facing a wall. Kneeling in the sand was uncomfortable and painful with small rough stones digging into my knees. I was struck in my lower back with a rifle butt when I shifted my weight from one knee to the next. Whoever it was that struck me also told me not to move, interjected with expletives.

Everything went blank from there on until I was assisted into a helicopter. I must have been in a daze up to that point because I did not hear or even see when the helicopter arrived. It took off and after about ten minutes we landed and were taken by vehicle to what turned out to be our destination. Before leaving the vehicle, I was blindfolded and led into a building where I was once again frisked.

Someone, I presumed a doctor, conducted a brief physical examination and pronounced that I was fit; for what I could not tell. I was left standing for about half an hour when the blindfold was removed. I was pushed against a wall and told to wait. I wondered what else I could have done. Even with all that had gone on and the trauma I had experienced I could not help but smile at the exercise of authority over the helpless. I thought that some people are puffed up with their sense of power, particularly when they had the upper hand.

The moment of reflection on the abuse of power passed as I was led to an office. Behind the single desk in the room sat an Officer and on the desk was an open folder with several sheets of paper in it. The handcuffs were removed and were replaced with an identity tag. The Officer began the interrogation by asking me my name, nationality, employer and what I was doing in Mogadishu. The interrogation was quite professionally done; no anger or resentment in the Officer's tone. I was unnerved by what I had suffered up to that point, but I answered the questions, and then I asked one of my own.

"Why were we assaulted and brought here when our identities had already been confirmed from the documents we provided?"

The Officer did not respond to my question, but continued with his interrogation.

"Why were you and your colleagues in that house?"

I had made up my mind that the exercise was futile, and decided not to answer any more questions. I told the Officer what I had decided and also said that if he really wanted to confirm our identities he should contact UNOSOM Security. Neither of us spoke for a few minutes. I just stood there alternately staring at the Officer, the walls, the ceiling and back to him again. I assume that he kept his eyes on me because each time I looked at him his gaze was always fixed on me.

After a few minutes, the Officer gestured to someone standing behind me. He came, and led me to an adjacent room where the other detainees, except Larry, were sitting on the floor. I was also told to sit next to them, but no conversation was allowed. About half an hour later, a soldier took me back to the "interrogation room". The Officer ordered a soldier to remove my identity tag, and he told me that I was free to go.

"Go where?" Was my response since I did not know where I was or where I was supposed to go?

At the same time, Larry and the others were brought into the room, arrangements were made for a vehicle to take us to UNOSOM II Compound. While we were waiting for transportation, there was a metamorphosis; our jailers had become our friends. They apologized for what had happened and offered us coffee, rolls and cigarettes. We did not accept their apology or their hospitality. I was too shaken up to eat, and too angry for all they had put us through to overlook what had transpired. I understood that mistakes were inevitable in the Somalia context, but to be subjected to battering, even after our identities were confirmed, was inexcusable.

A high ranking officer also came to see us. He apologized for the mistake that was made when the soldiers attacked our building, and what we had been made to endure. We later found out that he was Colonel Garrison, Commanding Officer of Task Force (TF)

Rangers, and that the Rangers had only recently arrived in the country with the specific mission to capture General Aidid.

During my interrogation and indeed long before that, I was experiencing debilitating pain in my wrists, arms and lower back. Sand was also lodged under my eye lids. I assumed that occurred when the helicopter landed to take us to the military barracks. My arms were handcuffed behind my back otherwise I would have shielded my eyes from the swirling sand. I asked to see a doctor, so the Officer ordered the driver of our transport to take me to the Swedish hospital that was next door to where we had been held. A nurse treated my swollen wrists and hands, saline washed my eyes, and gave me aspirin for pain, but no treatment could have assuaged the humiliation and degradation I suffered.

It was approximately eight hours from the time the assault began, the detention, interrogation, and medical treatment to the time when we were finally driven to UNOSOM II compound, which was adjacent to the US military encampment. We had no idea we were so close to UNOSOM II officials who could have made an on-site inspection to verify our identities if they had been asked. But, for whatever reason, our captors did not see fit to investigate what we had told them from the beginning.

Shortly after arriving at UNOSOM II compound, my colleagues and I made a verbal report to Admiral Howe and the UN Security team about the assault. After that, we attended a military debriefing with several officers of varying ranks. One of the officers repeated what we had been told earlier, that our building was not the target. The building the Rangers intended to hit was next door. It housed a French NGO that was providing excellent medical and famine relief services to Somalis. I never understood why that organization came into the cross hairs of the Rangers. And, of course, no further explanation was given except that the NGO was aiding and abetting Aidid's militia.

We left UNOSOM II compound early that afternoon and went to our residence where we were reunited with Nawal. She was in good shape considering the ordeal she had endured. A Somali family, living next door, came to her rescue after the soldiers left, and remained with her until we returned. They were truly good Samaritans who took compassion on a defenseless woman.

Except for the front door hanging on its hinges, the outside of the building looked pretty much as it did the day before the assault. It was the inside that told an entirely different story. The smoke from the explosions had not totally dissipated, and there was still the smell of cordite in the air. Not only were all the inner doors blown off their hinges, but several walls were completely demolished.

The televisions, refrigerator and stove were damaged beyond repair. I was amazed that we were not killed, and only came away with considerable bruises and wounded egos. The psychological damage and physical impairment such as sciatica, post-traumatic stress and diminished immune system would come later. In the meantime, all of us suffered from headaches, back pain, temporary paralysis of the arms and legs and insomnia.

Word soon got out that the Rangers had assaulted a United Nations' building. The media was there when we returned to our residence and pressed us for details on what had happened: Why had a UN office come under attack? We did not respond to the queries, but referred the reporters to Admiral Howe's office and the US military for answers. We were, therefore, perplexed at first, then furious when we heard UNOSOM's news release on CNN that night. Not only did that august body blame us for being in a restricted area, but they also cast aspersions on our character.

According to UNOSOM II, we knew that the area where we were staying was out of bounds, but disregarded explicit instructions to keep out. No such instruction was propagated. To add insult to injury, rumors were circulated that commercial quantities of qat, and large sums of cash were found in our residence. Those statements insinuated that we were drug dealers. I am sure that qat must have been on the premises; after all it was not a banned substance. Somalis of all levels chewed qat. The guards got paid and, as a matter of course, they bought qat for their personal use.

The officials at UNOSOM II even went further. They reported that we had used the HF radios in the office, the night before the attack, to transmit messages to Aidid. They never explained what information we could possibly have had that would have been of interest to Aidid. We were not privy to military secrets and troop movements. We did not know Admiral Howe had requested the services of the US Rangers; that they had been deployed and had, in fact, arrived in the country about a week before the attack on our building.

We had no idea what was being communicated between the UN Secretary General in New York and the Special Representative in Somalia about Aidid. The allegation about passing on information to Aidid was, therefore, ludicrous. I do not think Aidid would have been interested in the only type of information we could have provided, such as how much water the Water Project was supplying to residents of Mogadishu, including UN staff and the US military. Future development plans, support for livestock export or other technical assistance projects could not have been of interest to Aidid.

The White House also picked up the refrain and along with the UN Secretariat, lauded the successful mission of the Rangers. If the mission was so successful, what was the outcome? The only tangible result was the destruction of UNDP property and the assault on

UNDP staff. I believed that it would have been so much better if UNOSOM II had just told the plain truth, without embellishments and moved on. They should have said that the raid was a mistake and that steps were being taken to ensure that the same thing would not happen again. Instead, they doubled down, and perpetrated a lie that only served to alienate people in the International Community who knew the truth. The result was suspicion and mistrust of UNOSOM II and the US military.

The Resident Representative, Peter Schuman was not in Mogadishu during the raid. He returned the following day and made several attempts to meet with US military officials and Admiral Howe. Peter also tried to meet with whoever could have assisted in resolving the problem that had the potential to disrupt UNDP's input in Somalia's recovery activities. Eventually, Peter was able to arrange a meeting with a captain in the US Military Intelligence Unit. What came out of that meeting was appalling, and explained how inept military intelligence gathering was in Somalia. The mistake was reminiscent of the one the US military made when it acted on false information on July 12.

According to the Captain the area, including the Water Project compound, had been under clandestine helicopter and on the ground surveillance for several weeks before the raid. On one occasion, the crew of one of the helicopters became suspicious when they observed a large number of drums in the compound they later identified as the Water Project. On subsequent flights, they noticed that several drums had mysteriously disappeared only to be returned a few days later.

They had also noticed that the earth in the compound had been turned. This suggested, to the aerial observers, that the residents of the compound were trying to hide something. Perhaps they had incriminating documents that they were trying to conceal. The explanations that caused so much suspicion could be compared to a drowning man clutching at straws. I was embarrassed for the Officer who was obviously regurgitating nonsensical drivel that even he did not believe. I would have let the matter drop not wanting to compound his discomfort, but had to respond for the record.

I reminded the Officer that Mogadishu did not provide electricity to the residents of the city. Each compound had generators that used diesel and replenished their stock of diesel as the need arose; that was why there were drums in the compound. I also told him that if we wanted to hide documents, we would certainly not bury them, but would have made a bonfire thereby ensuring their immediate destruction. The Officer was further humiliated when I asked him if he were aware of the agreement between the US military and the Water Project. The understanding was that the military would provide diesel for the generators at the water pumping sites and the Water Project would provide the military with water.

I also asked him if the aerial observers had ever seen US military vehicles in the Water Project compound, or the massive GI tent that was pitched in the compound for weeks on end. The tent had only been removed about a week before the assault. Another fact was that UN flags were prominently displayed in the compound and plastered on the roofs of the office and residence buildings. It was hard to conceive that the people who gathered intelligence could have been so incompetent as to miss those clues. The only plausible conclusion was that the Rangers had made a mistake, in the dark, and were too embarrassed to admit it.

Immediately following the incident, UNDP New York informed us that one of its Associate Administrators was looking into the matter. We were also told that we should remain in Mogadishu because the Associate Administrator was planning a visit and was in the process of arranging meetings with Admiral Howe and ranking military officers. Weeks passed; the hype faded, and when we inquired about the status of the visit, we were informed us that the subject had been dropped. No further information was available.

We had remained in Mogadishu because of the proposed visit and expectation that the matter could have been resolved. After being told that the visit had been called off, we determined that it was pointless to remain in Somalia. However, the Rangers would not return our identity papers, claiming they were lost. Notwithstanding what they said, we demanded the return of our papers. One day around the middle of September, the documents mysteriously appeared on the desk in our makeshift office. No explanations were given, and we did not ask any questions. A few days after the papers were returned, my colleagues left for Nairobi.

I did not go with them because I had a problem. The mere thought of getting on an airplane sent me into a panic; sweating profusely, increased heart rate and uncontrolled tremors throughout my body. It did not occur to me, at the time, I was suffering from a severe malady, otherwise known as Post Traumatic Stress Disorder or PTSD. Peter Schuman knew of my dilemma, but was unable to convince me that I needed therapy.

Several weeks passed without my making any serious effort to leave Mogadishu. I was hampered from getting around because of continued unrest in the streets, but I stayed although the symptoms of PTSD increased with each passing day. That was how I came to be in Mogadishu on October 3, 1993 when two Black Hawk helicopters were shot down in the incident that became known as "Black Hawk Down."

I knew something momentous was going on, commencing around 1600 hours because of the high-pitched, excited chatter on the field radio. I did not have any details of the fire fight until after the fact. As if by pre-arrangement everyone in International

Community stayed indoors when it became apparent that a military operation was underway. No one wanted a repeat of the July 12 incident when innocent people were killed. Uppermost in my mind were the young American soldiers I had met at the Water Project and at their military camp. For some unfathomable reason, I could not shake the visual of dead bodies being dragged through the streets of Mogadishu.

The disrespect Aidid's militia had shown to the bodies of the dead Americans was not surprising, but only added to the disgust I already felt against the thugs masquerading as soldiers. Of course, that kind of inhumane treatment of the dead is not relegated to Somalis alone. There are well known cases how American soldiers mistreated enemy dead under similar circumstances. The difference in the actions of the two opposing forces is that desecrating the dead is standard practice for Somalis. No consequences are attached to such actions with the result that they are repeated with some degree of regularity.

Almost a month before the Black Hawk incident, a company of Nigerian soldiers was ambushed at a checkpoint and seven of them were killed. They were Muslims, just like the Somalis, but their bodies were desecrated, children poking the bodies with sticks, laughing while they committed such atrocities. The Somali philosophy in their treatment of the dead is quite clear. "The enemy is the enemy", and is treated as such dead or alive. .

There are the "Rules of Engagement" that order the behavior of the US military. Again, those regulations had sometimes been set aside out of expediency or in the heat of battle, but have not gone unpunished when they came to light.

No such rules existed in the Somali context. Peacekeepers always found themselves at a disadvantage when they were faced with the Somali concept of how wars are conducted. On one occasion, I witnessed Somali militia using women and children as shields as they engaged Peacekeepers in a fire fight. I was at the hotel near Kilometer Five in Mogadishu, when a crowd of women and children marched down the street protesting against the U.N. presence in Somalia. A contingent of Peacekeepers tried to break up the demonstration, but they came under fire from Aidid's militia who were hiding behind the women and children. The Peacekeepers had to retreat to the grounds of the hotel where I had a clear view of the activities in the street below. The demonstrators passed the hotel, and made their way to the airport where they quickly dispersed. Fortunately, no one was killed in that encounter.

More chatter and explosion about a mile from my vantage point brought me back to the present. I became quite agitated as if I were in the heat of battle. It was obvious that I was having a panic attack and there was nothing I could have done about it. I had to control my emotions and wait for definitive news about what was going on and, just as important, what was the outcome.

The soldiers involved in the Black Hawk Down incident acquitted themselves well in the battle with Aidid's militia and his supporters. However, they were placed in an untenable situation when they were ordered to engage the enemy on their territory without adequate equipment, and were outnumbered as bullets and rockets rained down on them.

American men and women are often placed in harm's way on the orders of politicians, and are at the mercy of bureaucrats who make bad decisions, sometimes with dire consequences. I was reminded of a government official who was criticized because the troops in Iraq were being killed and injured by IUDs. They did not have the equipment that would have given them some measure of protection. The official's response was:

"As you know, you go to war with the Army you have, not the Army you might want or wish to have at a later time."

That statement would be within the realm of reason if the USA had come under attack and had to defend herself. However, in the context of the Iraq war, the U.S. should have been prepared before initiating an attack on another country.

A similar situation presented itself in Somalia with soldiers being ill-equipped to carry out their mission. The Rangers' command had requested Abrams Tanks and Bradley armored vehicles when they were deployed to Somalia to capture General Aidid. However, the request was denied by the Clinton Administration. Many people, including military experts, believed that, if the request had been granted, fewer soldiers would have been killed. With proper armored support, the Rangers could have fought their way through the mob that attacked them, and many lives would have been saved on both sides.

Although the incident has been widely and, I believe, accurately reported I think a brief recap of salient points may be useful. On October 3, TF Rangers were ordered by Colonel Garrison to capture some of Aidid's top leaders who were known to be at the Olympic Hotel in Mogadishu. The hotel was located near the Bakaara Market, a densely populated area in the center of Aidid's territory with narrow streets and alleyways. The neighborhood was more like a maze with ill- defined entrances and exits to the many buildings in the area.

The mission commenced with an air assault on the target, and within a short time, twenty-four of Aidid's top leaders were captured. The Rangers came under heavy fire as they waited to be extracted from the combat zone. They fought back inflicting heavy casualties on their attackers and sustaining some casualties of their own. The ground convoy that was sent in to remove the Rangers and their prisoners were also attacked by Aidid's militia, and a mob of his supporters who lived in the area. During the engagement, two Black Hawk helicopters were shot down by Rocket Propelled Grenades.

The Rangers fought a running battle with Aidid's militia and an enraged mob, that joined the fight until the Rangers and their prisoners were finally extracted from the scene. During the battle that lasted for seventeen hours, 18 members of TF Rangers lay dead, and 84 were injured. It was estimated that some 500 Somalis were killed. The book "Black Hawk Down" by Mark Bowden provides an excellent account of the battle, including the capture of Chief Warrant Officer Durant.

I think it is pertinent to add some more information about the Clinton Administration's fault in undermining the efforts of the Rangers to capture Aidid, and what transpired after the incident on October 3-4. In addition to refusing to deploy the equipment the Commanding Officer requested, President Clinton had approved secret negotiations with Aidid, using former President Jimmy Carter as a Special Envoy. The negotiations were carried out at the same time the Rangers were actively seeking to apprehend Aidid. This may very well have sent confusing signals to Aidid and bolstered his refusal to negotiate with UNOSOM II.

The Rangers were prepared to complete their mission to capture Aidid. However the mission was aborted when President Clinton announced the withdrawal of US forces from Somalia. The announcement was made just five days after the Black Hawk incident. Two months later President Clinton ordered the release of the Somali prisoners, who had been captured during the first hour of the assault, and for which the Rangers had paid such a terrible price.

Aid workers were disappointed with the announced withdrawal of the Rangers from Somalia before they had finished the job they were sent to do. Everyone was looking forward to a period of stability to serve the Somali people in a peaceful climate without contending with General Aidid and his militia. That proved to be wishful thinking as Aidid and his militia continued their assault on their rivals. The streets became unsafe once more as the various groups vied for control of the city. The Peacekeepers kept out of the fray unless they had to defend themselves when they were attacked.

A Jordanian colleague, Dr. Ahmad Salah, summed up our collective thoughts when he commented on the perception of weakness that the Americans displayed as soon as they suffered a setback. He recalled similar actions by previous administrations, going back to October 1983, when President Reagan withdrew American forces from Beirut after some 240 American servicemen were killed at the hands of a suicide bomber. Beirut and Mogadishu were two disparate situations, but were linked to the apparent unwillingness of American politicians to face criticism from the American public. So the politicians capitulated, even when forging ahead to reach the objectives would have paid dividends in the end.

After President Clinton called off the search, Aidid was free to move about Mogadishu with the knowledge that he was not being pursued by the Rangers. He became even more belligerent and continued to incite unrest in the country. He refused to deal with the United Nations and take part in the reconciliation process. He boycotted a conference the Ethiopians had sponsored in Addis Ababa in early December 1993. He was later persuaded, by entities we can only guess at, to attend the conference on an American military aircraft, under the protection of American soldiers. The irony of American soldiers providing transport for Aidid, and protecting him is overwhelming.

Detente with the UN and the Americans was established after the conference. The Americans withdrew from Somalia in May 1994 and UNOSOM II completed its mission in March 1995. General

Mohammad Farrah Aidid died in August 1996 from wounds he sustained in battle.

Today, Somalia has little to show for all the money expended and the sacrifices that were made by so many people to alleviate the suffering of the Somali people. The magazine FP (Foreign Policy) estimates that about $55 billion has been spent since 1991. During the period November 1992 to October 1993, some sixty Peacekeepers were killed, including twenty-seven Americans. An estimated 3,000 Somalis died as a result of military action between Aidid's militia and UN Peacekeepers. Lawlessness and the upsurge of terrorism are still evident today some 20 years later. Somali pirates are infamous for commandeering ships in the Indian Ocean; and religious fanatics, including groups such as al-Shabaab, impose their will on the Somali people. Somalia is today experiencing the worse famine the world has seen in twenty years. Only God knows where and how it will end.

After the Rangers damaged our residence we were housed by WFP until we could find suitable accommodation. A week later, I rented a small house near the airport, on a temporary basis, until the building I had leased earlier was ready for occupancy. The house was located in a dead end street. That was not an ideal situation from a security standpoint. We had informed UNOSOM II about our concerns, and were assigned a Nepalese contingent to protect us. The assignment of the guards had relieved some of our anxieties.

However, the Officer in charge of our guards also pointed out another security concern. The guards did not have a clear view of the main road from their surveillance perch on the roof of our building. Not being able to see what was going on the main road, from the roof of our building, almost cost me my life, and the lives of the people who were in the vehicle with me.

One day as I left the office and turned into the main road, my vehicle was riddled with bullets from two groups firing at each other from opposite sides of the road. My driver was hit in his left arm, but he managed to maintain control of the vehicle though blood was spurting from the wound. As soon as we were out of range of the shooting, the driver stopped, and one of the guards made a tourniquet to stem the flow of blood. Another guard drove the vehicle to the airport that was a little less than a mile up the road, and took the driver to the medical center inside the terminal. A doctor attended to his wound and he was released about an hour later.

The shooting incident was the third time I came close to being killed. My fear of being on an airplane was forgotten in the aftermath of the latest episode of violence. After making sure that the driver was doing well, I went to the despatcher's office and booked a flight for Nairobi for the following day. The flight was scheduled for 0800 hours but my anxiety level was so high that I was at the airport at 0600 hours. Before the flight took off I started to panic, but managed to keep my fear under control and, in that state of mind, I made a vow never to return to Somalia.

9

Post-Traumatic Stress

*"Minds are like parachutes
they only function when they are open."*
Thomas Dewar

The flight to Nairobi was uneventful except that my fear of flying was still very evident. I panicked each time there was turbulence, no matter how mild. An additional factor that contributed to my discomfort was my thoughts about what happened after my encounter with the Rangers. I had recurring nightmares, frequently waking up at 0300 hours frightened, disoriented and sweating profusely. Every time that happened I was transported, if only temporarily, to the morning of August 30. Sometimes I went back to sleep immediately when I realized that I was only dreaming. At other times, I stayed awake until sunrise reliving that frightening event.

The assault and its aftermath had severe consequences and affected my health at a later date. I did not realize that the trauma was so intense, because my mind had blocked out some aspects of it. However my subconscious could not be silenced or rather it would not allow me to escape from the consequences of the ordeal. One of its manifestations was that it prevented me from functioning with any degree of consistency. My mind was closed, and I did not even know it. Strange things began to happen like day dreaming in the middle of the day as my mind wandered to the events of August 30. Another example was that I found it extremely frightening to be in any confined space; even so I did not connect that with my recent traumatic experience.

There were some things I noticed that were out of the norm. I was extremely jumpy, nervous and would actually break out in perspiration at the slightest indication that I was not in control over any situation in which I was involved. Getting into elevators was definitely out of the question, since it was not uncommon for the confounded contraptions to make stops that were not ordered or, worse still, between floors. Imagine not being able to be confined in an elevator for a few seconds; that explained why being on an airplane, for hours, was so terrifying for me.

I had also become very uncomfortable in a crowd, if people were armed or not but, especially if they were armed. I was unnerved by the sound of weapons being discharged and could no longer tolerate the boom of artillery. Either one of those things would alarm me, the precursor to a full-fledged panic attack. Helicopters were a special menace. The drone of approaching Black hawks or Cobras terrified me, and I would consciously seek to get out of range of the beating rotors, and the inevitable swoosh of rockets being fired.

I knew, intellectually, that something was wrong, but would not admit it, particularly to my colleagues. The most damning thing was my refusal to acknowledge the change all those things had brought about in me. After the incident with the Rangers and before they left for Nairobi, my associates noticed the dramatic change and one, in particular, Nawal, tried to intervene, tried desperately to get me to focus on what I was doing. Critical decisions, such as determining safe zones in case of an urgent need to evacuate the city, were kept pending. I could not make up my mind about simple tasks, not to mention the difficult ones. This was a dangerous situation where lives were in jeopardy, and depended on clear and decisive action.

Those who worked with me saw that an immediate intervention, by a qualified therapist, was necessary. Someone had to unravel my mind to determine precisely what was locked up in the subconscious. I kept insisting that all was well, and that nothing truly bothered me. Taking into account what I had experienced, those two statements by themselves were sufficient indication that I needed help.

A few days after arriving in Nairobi, I was sitting at my desk when a woman rapped on the open door and asked for information on UNDP's role in Kenya. I told her to see to the Administrative Officer for Kenya, since my knowledge of the Kenya operations was limited. However, I could provide information on Somalia, which was much more interesting. The visitor responded that we could have a discussion about Somalia at another time, but her current mandate centered on Kenya. And that was that, at least so I believed.

Later on I found out that the person who was inquiring about Kenya, Susan Kinloch, knew precisely who I was. Susan's intention was to engage me in conversation that did not include Somalia initially. She was a trauma specialist, and was very much aware that any misstep about Somalia would trigger a negative response or worse. So she pretended disinterest in Somalia, and talked about Kenya instead. Even as she talked about Kenya, she was sizing me up, trying to figure out how to approach her potential patient. UNDP New York and the Peter Schuman had warned Susan about my recalcitrance, my unreasonable defiance in not wanting to accept help. It was almost as if I were prepared to do battle with anyone who suggested that I needed therapy.

After Susan left, I gave no further thought to what was said. I continued with plans to travel to Djibouti the following day to withdraw $300,000 from the bank. The trips to Djibouti had become a bi-monthly affair to fund the operation in Mogadishu.

There were no banks, credit unions, money exchange offices in Mogadishu, or any other part of Somalia for that matter. The financial institutions in Mogadishu resided in Bakaara Market, where traders supplied all commodities for Mogadishu; meat, fish, fruits, vegetables, clothing, guns, you name it, and yes Somali shillings. That was still the currency used in trade, and anyone doing business in Mogadishu went to Bakaara Market to obtain shillings. As I thought about shillings, I was reminded of my first encounter with the official currency of Somalia.

Shortly after arriving in Mogadishu in November 1992, I had met Jim Slater, the Water Project Manager for the first time. He greeted me, as I walked in his office, in his booming voice.

"Welcome to Mogadishu, this hell hole of a place!" Jim said. "We certainly need someone with your expertise to help us sort out this administrative mess. Incidentally, do you see anything unusual in this room?"

I looked around, and noted what looked like money neatly stacked against the wall. Next to the money was the largest safe I had ever seen in such a small office.

"I would think that the money stacked against the wall should be in the safe. But I am sure there is a valid reason for whatever is unusual about that," I had responded.

Jim walked over to the safe dialed the combination, and with a click, he swung the door open. The safe was full of paper, pens, pencils, ink, staplers and staples and every imaginable type of stationary one could think about.

"Have you ever been in a place where stationary is at a premium and more important than currency?" Jim asked me.

"Yes, Angola," was my response.

My reverie ended abruptly as I became aware of a figure standing in the doorway.

"Me again," Susan Kinloch said. "However, this time I would like to ask about mundane things, like where is the best place to have lunch in Nairobi?"

Susan was an expert at dealing with confused minds. She told me she had heard about some really quaint restaurants in Nairobi. I had agreed and before I knew what was happening, we were sitting down to lunch at a restaurant about two blocks from the office.

The discussion was quite innocuous at first. We discussed the Kenya weather, among the best in the world. We talked about safaris, the Kikuyus, the Masai, other ethnic groups, and the reason why UNDP was not housed in the UN compound in Nairobi. We then talked about an incident that had traumatized the UN community in Nairobi about two months earlier.

A U.N. staff member was accosted at the gate to the United Nations compound by a gunman, who demanded the key for the staffer's brand-new car. When he refused to give it up, the gunman shot him dead on the spot and escaped with the vehicle in view of other staff members who were arriving at work at the same time. That incident sent a tremor of fear throughout the entire U.N. community. Unbeknownst to me, was the fact that my lunch companion, and another colleague of hers, had been sent to Nairobi by the United Nations in New York to counsel staff in Nairobi over the incident. Susan's consulting firm had also been contracted to provide therapy to UNDP staff who were assaulted by the Rangers.

Car hijackings were not unusual in Nairobi, and for that reason, the United Nations had gone to extensive lengths and expense to council staffers on how they should respond in the event they were involved in a car hijack. A few months before the incident at the gate to the UN compound, a staff member of another international organization had been shot and killed outside a friend's home. In that incident, the vehicle was equipped with a damper.

As the staff member left the home he was visiting, he was approached by a gunman who demanded the keys for the vehicle. The victim did not argue, but handed over the keys immediately. However, when the gunman tried to start the car, it stalled. He calmly got out of the vehicle and shot the victim once in the head. Before bystanders could react to what had just happened, another vehicle pulled up and whisked the gunman away.

That incident had affected the international community at its core. Hijackings of vehicles had become a way of life in many parts of Africa. That was particularly true for countries with unstable governments. Initially the incidences had always been directed at businessmen, high ranking civil servants and the affluent. The gangsters had never dared to attack AID Agencies, or even the lowly non-government organizations that provided some essential service, mostly in the health field. All that changed when the hijackers tested the waters, and took the first vehicle belonging to an AID Agency at gun point. Sadly nothing happened to apprehend the criminals, only a tame outcry from the people who lost their vehicle and an even weaker response from the government. So car hijackings became a typical way of life that culminated in the murder of a staffer at the gate of the United Nations compound.

Susan introduced Somalia into our conversation by asking about incidences of cars being stolen at gunpoint in Somalia. The introduction led to a discussion about the famine, lawlessness civil war, and the US Military. Without any prompting from Susan, I went into details about what I had experienced, including the assault by the US Rangers.

It was at that point that the missing piece in the puzzle, which was locked away in my subconscious, came to the surface, fitted perfectly into the picture, and the closed door was unlocked. The flood gates opened, and I recalled the incident that caused the trauma as if it had happened just yesterday. So the story surfaced. I told Susan all that had transpired, from the time of the first explosions, to the time when we were taken to the military compound. I had not delved into any details about my experiences before speaking with Susan. Perhaps giving voice to what had happened was the key to my deliverance.

I talked about being taken by the Rangers from our residence to the compound down the street, and that I was separated from my colleagues. I was made to kneel facing a wall with the Rangers at my back; wrists bound, blindfolded execution style and was told not to make a sound or move a muscle.

"We are the judges and executioners here, and we will decide your fate," one of the Rangers had said. "At least you will know where and when your end will come. You will be given sufficient time to prepare to meet your Maker; unlike the fate suffered by four of our colleagues who were mercilessly killed by a roadside bomb a few days ago."

The fear that rippled through me as the Ranger spoke was worse than the fear I felt when the building was being destroyed around us. The menace in the Ranger's voice was not a threat but was infused with a promise of things to come. As I knelt there, a shot rang out, and I was transported to another place. At the very moment the shot was heard, I felt a searing pain as the bullet ripped through my body shattering organs and exploding leaving a hole as big as my fist. I pitched forward and in my deluded state of mind, saw myself in a coffin with friends and family gathered around. People were wailing and crying, the sounds rising above the Pastor's voice as he gave the eulogy. Then it occurred to me that I could not be dead at all. Uncontrollable fear had taken hold of me, with the result that the mere cocking of a weapon mimicked the sound of it being discharged. I was relieved to find myself still kneeling, facing the wall and in the same position as when I was first brought to that desolate place.

I wondered why a weapon was being cocked, so I turned to look at my captors. My movement was again met with a sharp pain as one of the Rangers jammed the butt of his rifle into my lower back. It was a lesson in obedience. If you are told not to move, then you do not move. The pain was excruciating, but I did not make a sound thinking that would elicit another unwelcome response.

"We'll be taking you to our camp for interrogation in a few minutes," one of the Rangers said. "A helicopter will transport us, and if you know what is good for you, you will not give us any trouble otherwise we will hurt you **real bad**."

I had heard rumors of "accidents" while prisoners were being transported in helicopters—accidents in which prisoners had fallen out of the helicopter. Once more, I was consumed with dread and knew for sure that I would face the same fate. That was when I decided to speak, not thinking or caring what would come out of it. After all what could be worse than what had already happened or what was to come?

I reminded the Rangers that my colleagues and I had not given any trouble since we were taken into custody. We cooperated at every turn, had shown evidence of our identities, and yet we had been manhandled and physically assaulted. I told them that they had the upper hand; they had the weapons so why would anyone be stupid enough to resist?

I felt, unreasonably, that the more I spoke the longer it would take the helicopter to arrive. The longer that lasted then the inevitable would be delayed, the inevitable because, in my mind, my day of reckoning had arrived. It was as if I had reconciled myself to the fact that I would not see another sunrise. My family was uppermost on my mind, and I was saddened by the very thought that I would not see my wife and children again; that I would die in this God-forsaken place without loving and kindly faces around. Instead, I was surrounded by hostility, not only the hostility of my captors but the hostility of cannons booming in the distance; the hostility of the rattle of weapons being fired and exchanges being made by parties hostile to each other. My world was filled with hatred, suspicion and yes, hostility.

It seemed to me that I was in a daze and, in that state a profound calm enveloped me. I was resigned to my fate, and perhaps that was the source of the solace that encompassed me. I was aware of the Rangers standing behind me but at that time they did not pose a threat to me. The peace I felt within included them also. The Rangers did not pose a threat any longer and, to a certain extent, they were company in that desolate place. I did not want to be alone, not even under the circumstance.

"Your English is extremely good," I heard someone say.

I told the Rangers that English was my mother tongue and that I was from Belize. After that exchange, there was a dramatic change in their demeanor and general attitude towards me. There was a long pause, and then I felt gentler hands lifting me up and voices that were no longer hostile telling me that I was being taken to rejoin my colleagues. According to my captors, they had no choice but to take all of us to army headquarters for interrogation by the army's intelligence unit, although our identities had been established.

That incident was the missing piece to the puzzle, and it allowed me to see everything that had happened in a different perspective. During those critical minutes when I felt that my life hung in a balance, that was tipping slowly to my being killed, my mind had blocked the entire incident; the part where I was sure I would die, and the part when I knew I would live to see another day. Everything went, and, as a result, my subconscious placed everything on hold. I became irrational; sounds triggered fear and anxiety, and I was slowly spiraling out of control until I spoke with Susan Kinloch. Although I had benefited from the therapy, I still had a long way to go to rid myself of my fear of flying, of helicopters and claustrophobia. I was also frustrated with UNDP for not resolving my issues with UNOSOM II and the Rangers.

A few days after my session with Susan, I took two weeks off to visit my family in New York and to speak with the responsible parties at UNDP headquarters. I had also planned to ask for a transfer to another country, even though I had only been in Somalia for one year. I was actually expected to be there for at least two years, but given my traumatic experience, I knew my request would have been favorably considered.

I arrived in New York around October 20, 1993. A few days later, I had a meeting with the Director of the Arab Bureau, and the Associate Administrator of UNDP who was supposed to solve my issue with UNOSOM II and the US military. I was not then, or am I now, in the habit of using foul language, but I lost it at one point in the meeting. The Associate Administrator told me, that if I insisted on having the UN resolve the matter with its office in Somalia, I and my colleagues would be held responsible for the damage to UNDP property for being in a place that was designated as off limits. I could not believe my ears and let loose with a barrage of colorful invectives that would have shamed the devil.

We had gone to great lengths to explain why we were at the Water Project residence at the time of the attack. More importantly, we had provided proof that no instruction had been given, designating the area as a restricted zone. After calming down, I told the Associate Administrator that I was prepared to continue with my case against UNOSOM II, and the US military regardless of charges that might be brought against me. My colleagues were free to choose for themselves whether or not they wanted to continue. The Associate Administrator told me that the matter was being taken under advisement, and that I would be informed accordingly.

A few days after the meeting, I went to see a friend who was assigned to New York and was a member of the administration's inner circle. We had worked under difficult conditions in Sierra Leone and had developed a close friendship based on trust and respect.

He told me, in confidence, that the UNDP official who was responsible for liaising with the United Nations had been persuaded not to pursue the matter. Some years earlier, the same official was prosecuted before a New York court for sexual harassment. The UN had invoked diplomatic immunity for the official, and, while it had made a monetary settlement, the official himself had been held blameless. He was neither required to pay restitution nor did he lose his job, but continued his employment as if nothing had happened.

He must have forgotten that he was under obligation to the UN for favors rendered to him in the past. When the subject of Somalia came up, the official was told to drop it or face the consequences of the sexual harassment charge. Self-preservation had taken precedence over other people's welfare and explained why the matter was shelved. It was pointless to proceed, so I dropped the matter, but insisted, even more strenuously, on a transfer out of Somalia.

Several spots were immediately available, including the post of Operations Manager in The Yemen and a similar post in Liberia. I refused both assignments outright. I was not prepared to be posted to another country with difficult living conditions. I was advised to return to Nairobi and continue with my work until a more suitable assignment became available.

Once those decisions were taken, I continued with my plan to spend some time with my family. My wife and I had also decided that she would accompany me to Nairobi, to shop for Kenyan artwork for a business in African art she had planned on starting. I figured it would take about a month to hand over to my successor, then we would be on our way to shop, and visit friends in Ethiopia, South Africa and Zimbabwe until a new assignment was arranged. Unfortunately, things did not work out as planned

We arrived in Nairobi in early November, and a week later I went to Mogadishu for one last time, even though I had made a solemn oath never to go back there again. The trip only lasted a few days during which I met with UNDP key staff and officials from other agencies. The day before I was to return to Nairobi, I was invited by some of the drivers and guards I had worked with, to have tea with them. I must have come in contact with a carrier of some deadly disease or, perhaps, I went against one of the first suggestions made to me when I arrived in Mogadishu a year earlier. Do not drink unpasteurized camel's milk or mix it with any beverage such as tea.

10

A Killer Disease

*"Treasure the love you receive above all
It will survive long after your good health have vanished"*
Og Mandino

About a week after returning to Nairobi, Raquel saw something different in my eyes that caused her some level of concern. She had always been attuned to me, and knew something was wrong when she noticed a change in my demeanor and in the color of my eyes.

"Your eyes are a muddy brown," she observed one morning as I was preparing to go to work.

I was in a hurry, preoccupied with thoughts about the dire situation in Mogadishu; and my colleagues still working there. I did not want to hear anything about eyes, muddy or not. So I responded with the impatience that was so typical of me in those days.

"Why are you looking at my eyes? There is nothing wrong with them." I told her.

"That is because you are unaware of your own body and the changes that any observant person sees," was her response.

She realized that was not the time for any discourse or argument about eye discoloration. She knew that I was late for an appointment, so she let the subject drop as I shrugged off her concerns, kissed her absent-mindedly and left.

A few days later, I complained about a splitting headache that would not go away no matter how many aspirin I took. I became irritable, and within a day or so, I had lost my appetite. Then along came a fever that was the strangest malady I had ever experienced. Raquel thought about our discussions over the years, about childhood illnesses, and the fact that I had fevers as a child, but never as an adult; although I was exposed to dengue fever, malaria, hepatitis, and other viruses that stressed the body to its limits. When I was on assignment in other places, people around me came down with dengue and malaria, but I did not contract those illnesses. Raquel recalled her bout with malaria during our assignment to Sierra Leone and how sick she had been. Then a few weeks later, Melanie, one of our daughters, came down with the same deadly fever.

There was also the incident in Angola when a friend contracted cerebral malaria and her life hung in the balance for days. Raquel recollected being scared out of her wits, not only for our friend and our friend's family, but more so for her own. She remembered berating herself for agreeing to an assignment in a place like Angola, exposing the family to war and pestilence. Our friend recovered, and the dangers associated with disease and illnesses receded into the distance as time went by.

Angola and what happened there came poignantly to mind as the days passed by, and my fever did not recede or abate but increased in intensity. Homemade remedies and over the counter medications from the drugstore in Yaya Center had no effect in cooling my fever-racked body. After two days without any let up in the strength of the fever, I went to see one of the United Nations designated physicians for Kenya.

Dr. Rhys, a Tropical Disease Specialist, studied in the United Kingdom but had honed his skills in tropical disease medicine, in Kenya. He had extensive experience in malaria diagnosis, care, research and prevention. At first, he thought that I had contracted malaria, but after seeing the results of blood and urine tests he concluded that was not the case. The doctor was also concerned about the complaint I registered about a consistent pain, slight but persistent, in my lower abdomen. The concern turned into a low-level of alarm when, a few days later, the results from several other tests came back that there was not a diagnosis for the fever and pain.

The doctor admitted me to the Nairobi Hospital that same day for observation. Other tests were performed, including abdominal scans and, without my permission, one for AIDS. All the test results were negative. However, the fever continued relentlessly, even as the doctor and his staff worked anxiously to diagnose the problem. In addition to the fever and the pain, I had become confused and could not follow the simplest instructions. Therefore, Dr. Rhys made sure that Raquel was present for all consultations. She too had noticed my dilemma and was deeply concerned about what was happening to me.

My hospital room was dull and uninviting. The walls needed a fresh coat of paint which would have done wonders to lift my spirits. Added to that was the discomfort of the bed. It seemed that it was made of straw or some other material that was equally uncomfortable. However, I was grateful that the room did not have any smells associated with hospitals, like disinfectant. The nurses, in their starched white uniforms and caps, went about their business briskly and exuded a sense of confidence in their abilities.

Raquel felt sad as she tried to make me comfortable for as long as I had to be in the hospital. She had decided that we would leave

Nairobi as soon as possible. For some unfathomable reason, she felt a sense of doom, and wanted us to return to New York. There was no concrete reason for the feeling of unease that permeated her deepest thoughts. Somehow she felt that I would not get well until I received treatment in the USA. She had ditched our travel plans to Ethiopia and Southern Africa and her dreams of starting a business in African art; at least for the time being.

Dr. Rhys, his associates and nurse provided excellent care. The hospital was, to all appearances, well-run and staffed by friendly and efficient professionals. However, Raquel could not shake her unease, particularly when it was time to leave me in the hospital at night and go back to our apartment. At times she felt that her unease at leaving me was unwarranted, that I would be alright. At other times she was plagued with the feeling that things would go wrong when she was not around.

Thanksgiving was just a few days away when I was admitted to the hospital. We had planned to celebrate the holiday with a friend from South Africa, but we discarded those plans when I became ill. Raquel was hard-pressed to leave me alone in a drab hospital room while she was at dinner with friends. She could not picture herself in that scenario, so she decided that she would stay with me instead. However, just as adamantly as she insisted on not going to the party, I argued even more strenuously that she should get away from the hospital. I assured her that I would be alright, and would call her immediately, at the friend's home, if anything untoward occurred.

The following day Raquel consulted with Dr. Rhys on my progress. There was nothing new to report. It wasn't as if they were completely clueless. I was immunized against a number of diseases, including the typhoid bacteria, so, although typhoid anti-bodies were present in my blood, Dr. Rhys concluded that typhoid was not the problem.

For one week, the doctors tested, probed, and tested some more; but to no avail. The fever persisted, and I became weaker as the days passed. My main sustenance during those days was honey, morning, noon and night. I could not ingest anything else, and had to be forced to eat even that. My appetite deserted me altogether and, instead of the usual rumbling in my stomach signaling the need for food, the pain in my stomach increased in intensity indicating that something else was wrong.

After one week in the hospital, Dr. Rhys finally applied the Widal test. It is a blood test used to identify unknown antigens; blood with the unknown antigen is mixed with a known antibody, and, whether or not agglutination occurs, the test helps to identify the antigen. The result from the analysis showed a positive diagnosis of typhoid fever. The doctor determined that the fever was caused by a virulent strain of bacteria, Salmonella Serotype Paratiphi. The clinical presentation in my case encompassed the most troubling manifestation such as high fever, abdominal pain, vomiting, and constipation. As soon as Dr. Rhys made the diagnosis, he placed me under a strict protocol of antibiotics. Valuable time had passed without treatment that later proved to have been a monstrous mistake.

The doctor placed me in isolation immediately in another wing of the hospital. The room was somewhat like a suite in a hotel. It was large with a sitting area containing two comfortable couches and a television. Raquel was also allowed to stay with me. That was the best decision about my treatment up to that time.

My wife, always curious, took note of the corridor outside the room. She saw that there was no nurse's station, only a mini kitchen. Qualified nurses dispensed medicines, gave injections took notes and asked about patient's wellbeing during the day. However, nurses were not on the floors at night or were they available for consultation, except in the Emergency Room.

Late one night, a few days after treatment began; I complained that I was extremely cold. I asked Raquel for several blankets to get warm because I was shivering uncontrollably. She touched my forehead and passed her hand over me, using her wrist to test the intensity of the heat emanating from my body. As her hand rested on my abdomen a puzzled look came over her face—my abdomen was cold as ice while the rest of my body was burning up. And then it happened—my body went into shock. My eyes rolled back in their sockets as my body stiffened. Raquel knew that I was in urgent need of medical attention, so she shouted to an attendant, who was sleeping in the hallway, to get a doctor immediately.

"I will call the doctor, Miss Mama," the attendant said as she sped from the room.

Shortly after the attendant returned with the Emergency-Room doctor. He immediately took charge, and started to work feverishly to stabilize me because he saw that I was slipping away. The doctor knew that the brain had already kicked into high gear because the signals revealed that something was terribly wrong. This is what is commonly known as compensated shock, when the brain reroutes all the blood throughout the body to the heart, brain, lungs and kidneys, the most important organs in the body. It was almost too late when the doctor came because I had already progressed to the critical stage when the body goes into "decompensated shock". The bacteria were waging a battle against the healing effects of the antibiotics.

The doctor worked through the night, using steroids and his experience and skills to keep me from going into irreversible shock. While the doctor worked on me, Raquel paced the corridor outside the room waiting for word on my condition. Several hours later, in what seemed like an eternity to her, the doctor came out of the room, exhausted but triumphant, and explained the process I had just gone through.

"I apologize for not introducing myself before, but I could tell that your husband was slipping away fast. I had to take immediate and drastic steps to stabilize him. I am Dr. Kiambu, and I am the Resident responsible for the Emergency Room. It was providential that you were here because, without your intervention, your husband would have surely died."

After the doctor left, Raquel collapsed on the bed out of sheer exhaustion and fell asleep almost immediately when her head touched the pillow.

She awoke to the faint sound of someone calling her name and saw me smiling weakly at her. I was aware that something momentous had happened during the night, and wanted to know why there were so many people around me, and why they had such bright lights on as they milled around. It was obvious that I must have been hallucinating. Raquel tried to explain what had transpired but, before she had finished her first sentence, I was snoring slightly as I slipped into blissful sleep.

Raquel was glad for the respite, because she did not think she could have explained my close brush with death. She could not form the words to tell me that I had almost passed away in the night. She could not explain that if she were not in my room, at that critical moment to witness my distress and called for help, I would have been found cold and lifeless the following morning. As a general rule, it seemed that critically ill patients were not monitored during the night. It was most disconcerting to Raquel, and, the following day, she spoke to Dr. Rhys about that crucial part of my care.

Raquel concluded that she had to find a way to keep watch even if it meant hiring private nursing care. She even got into the habit of checking on me at all hours, especially at night when the ward was eerily silent, and traffic throughout the hospital was at a minimum. Her experience that night made her so paranoid that she did not trust leaving my side. The paranoia developed into an obsession that was to take its toll on her health. A few days after the incident when I almost died, the fever started to abate. I was still very weak and did not have any significant respite from the constant pain in my lower abdomen. Never-the-less, Dr. Rhys felt that I was better off recuperating at home than being in the hospital. Raquel agreed, and so I went home on December 12 with the admonition that any change in my condition was to be reported immediately to Dr. Rhys, no matter the time of day or night.

Our apartment, in the Yaya Apartment complex, was large and pleasant, towering above the buildings nearby. There was a magnificent view of a part of Nairobi, and the distant mountains provided a beautiful panoramic view of the area. It was certainly better than being in the hospital. Both of us had a feeling of well-being and some measure of contentment at being back in the apartment. I was on the mend; at least I did not have a fever, though the pain I complained about continued unabated. However, things were looking up.

Five days after my release from the hospital I relapsed, and came down with a fever that was even worse than I had experienced before. The setback took us by surprise, even though we were warned about such a possibility. An ambulance rushed me to the Emergency Room where Dr. Rhys met me. He was very concerned with my condition. He thought that I appeared to be much weaker than I should have been.

Raquel had made arrangements for us to fly to New York where, she felt, I would receive a diagnosis for the relentless pain in my lower abdomen. We were holding tickets to fly to New York via

Athens. However, Raquel changed the reservations to travel via London instead. She thought that London would have been the better transit stop, instead of Athens, if I became too ill to continue the last leg of the journey to New York. We were scheduled to leave Nairobi on December 18 but those plans had to be postponed because I was back in the hospital.

Up to that point I had not discussed in detail any aspect of the assault, and the PTSD that ensued. My wife knew what she had seen on television and what she had read in the newspapers. We had cursory discussions about the assault, but she felt that I relived the trauma each time I talked about them. However, although discussing it might have helped her understand what I was going through, she did not ask and I did not volunteer the information.

It was enough that I had to discuss my experiences in official circles. However, I would not tell my wife about them, particularly my fear of flying. I did not want to diminish my macho image in her eyes. I felt I would seem less manly, cowering in fear about something as simple as getting on an airplane. She did not know that flying terrified me; that I was a mental wreck during our flight from New York to Athens, and from Athens to Nairobi. Since I did not tell her what I was experiencing, she did not know she was placing more stress on my already overstressed body, by insisting that we fly to New York as soon as possible. Raquel had hoped that we would be in New York in time for Christmas. She felt that being there would certainly help to lift my spirits and, hopefully, help in the healing process. However, that was apparently not going to happen, given the fact that I was back in the hospital.

A few days later on December 20 the fever abated, and I was released from the hospital on the 21st. The doctor was cautiously optimistic that I was fit to take the 16-hour flight to New York. He had given Raquel advice about what she should do, including the names and telephone numbers of two Tropical Disease Specialists in London, in case I relapsed, or was unable to continue on the flight to New York. Raquel thanked the doctor for the information he gave her. She then made arrangements for us to leave Nairobi the following night December 22.

11

The Struggle to Leave Nairobi

Always remember that striving and struggle precede success
Even in the dictionary"
Sarah Ban Breathnach

The 22nd came, and when the driver arrived to take us to the airport, I begged off and told my wife that I could not endure the flights to London and New York. At that point, it was pointless to equivocate, to try to avoid talking about the real problem. It was time for me to explain my innermost feelings and fears. It was time to tell my wife more about the experiences that traumatized me and why, even after some therapy, I was not "cured". I even cried, tears of frustration at my inability to explain fully what I was going through; the fear I felt just thinking about getting on an airplane.

The following day December 23, as my wife was making arrangements to leave that night, I talked to her quietly, in hushed tones as if someone could overhear our conversation. I spoke as if I were divulging some state secret that could have devastating consequences. In fact, I just wanted to tell her, as best as I could, that the long seemingly endless trip to New York was out of the question.

I wanted to tell her that I was afraid of a number of things. She should know that I was not the macho guy I pretended to be, and was just as vulnerable to all the things someone facing the probability of death had to endure.

I was also preoccupied with my mortality and the legacy to my children, grandchildren, and those yet to be born. But instead of speaking about those things that were nearest my heart, I chickened out and talked instead about a small part of what happened in Somalia. I thought that some of those things would help my wife to understand why I was claustrophobic—why there was a reluctance to be closeted in a tube with wings that hurled through the air at some 500 miles per hour.

It was necessary to go into details about my experiences before and after the incident with the Rangers. The assault had produced the debilitating effects of Post-Traumatic Stress Disorder, for which I should have received more extensive treatment. Therapy had been offered, but I had refused at first because "I was okay". Then there was the encounter with Susan Kinloch that helped to unlock my mind that had been closed to a crucial aspect of my traumatic experience. However, I was still not well and needed more extensive treatment.

I wanted to explain my disenchantment with UNDP for not supporting my colleagues and me in the aftermath of the assault. Even as I was trying to hide my vulnerability, wanting to be strong when I felt the weakest in my entire life, I knew that the truth should come out. It was essential, not only for my wife but for my peace of mind, to come to terms with what was really happening to me. But, I shied away from what I feared was really happening, and that was that depression was setting in. Depression was not an easy subject to discuss, especially when it was personal. No one liked to admit they are suffering from, what people might regard, as some type of mental disease. It was better if I ignored my illness and be left alone to find a dark, quiet corner and sleep.

Therefore, rather than speaking about the real issues that, I believed, would have reduced me in the eyes of my wife, I thought that some of my experiences in Somalia would suffice. I felt that after telling my wife some of the things I went through, she would understand and ease off from trying to get me on an airplane. It did not matter that my body, weakened by typhoid fever and abdominal pain, was deteriorating by the day. Somehow the problem would go away, and I would be whole again. I knew that was wishful thinking, but at least it kept me from having to consider the reason for being terrified of flying.

I found a comfortable spot on the sofa where the pain in my lower back and abdomen was tolerable. The view of the mountain from the sofa was soothing, making it easier for me to relate a part of my story. It began by being cognizant of the many experiences that could have ended tragically, but for the Grace of God. I had realized from the time I accepted the assignment to Somalia that I was placing my life on the line, given the situation in the country and the job I was to perform.

That realization did not deter me from trying to make a positive contribution to the tragedy in Somalia. Knowing that there was the possibility I could be injured or killed was not the same as coming face to face with death. But before those events became realities, I felt that, although bad things could happen, I would be fine. Contracting some strange illness or being shot at did not come into the picture I envisaged. Those things happened to other people. Those possibilities soon became realities from the first day I set foot in Somalia when I came face to face with a sub-machine gun pointing at me.

Then there was the time when the vehicle in which a colleague and I were traveling, rounded a corner and landed in the middle of a fire fight with Aidid's militia and UNITAF. That was the scariest incident up to that point with bullets hitting our vehicle. Two bullets even penetrated its shell and were later found lodged in the seat my colleague had occupied a few minutes before being pushed to the floor of the vehicle by one of our guards.

The worse experience, before the Ranger attack, however, was my venture into the northern section of Mogadishu controlled by Ali Mahdi. Someone had suggested that UNDP should consider moving its operation to that part of the city, out of Aidid's sphere of influence. I thought the idea was ludicrous for several reasons, particularly from a security standpoint. However, first hand inspection was better than hearsay, so I and a prospective landlord ventured into the north one day with Hassan, and three guards.

North Mogadishu was once the pride of the country with its Arab architecture, and white washed buildings that glisten in the bright sunlight. Practically nothing of its past glory and beauty remained only bombed out buildings and deserted streets. There were check points at the Green Line, the boundary between the north and south, and there were check points at practically every turn as we navigated the rubble strewn streets.

The building we were to inspect came into view. Just as we drove up to the entrance, a vehicle with four men, armed with automatic pistols and assault rifles, came around the corner and blocked us from proceeding further. Long before we reached our destination, I had already made up my mind that, regardless of the condition of the building, renting it was out of the question. First of all, for security reasons, it was too far from the airport and the port. In case a general evacuation was ordered, those were the best avenues of escape from the Mogadishu. Secondly, navigating so many checkpoints was dangerous and time consuming. The appearance of the vehicle only confirmed what I had been thinking, but I said nothing at that time.

The vehicle just stopped and did not move, though the driver knew he was blocking our path. The owner of the building we came to inspect was about to address the driver of the other vehicle, but Hassan held up his hand and told him in a quiet voice not to say anything. The two drivers stared at each other for what seemed an inordinate amount of time. The minutes, at least it seemed like minutes, went by as tension rose, but no one moved. At long last, the other vehicle swerved around ours and sped down the street. Hassan explained that he was quite familiar with the area and knew how to deal with the armed thugs that terrorized the neighborhood. They used fear to intimidate anyone who crossed their paths. They were cowards and only confronted weaker targets. Since our vehicle carried superior weapons, it was unlikely that we would have been attacked.

I was just about to go off on Hassan for placing our lives in jeopardy when, without warning, a shell exploded about fifty yards from us. Not a word was spoken as we jumped out of the vehicle, and took cover in the nearest undamaged structure. We had noticed the building before and had commented on how pristine it looked compared to others in the area. Even the building I came to inspect had sustained some damage but not as extensive as most.

As we huddled together, staying away from windows, we counted some ten explosions. Some were close enough to send shudders through the building. We were listening trying to judge the distance, from our location, of each exploding shell, when we heard the unmistakable sound of screams coming from the rear of the building. No one wanted to move, but we could not ignore the sound of someone in distress. One of the guards was the first to act. As soon as he opened the door that was nearest to him we saw a man lying on the ground, grasping his leg that had been blown away just below the knee.

We were all in shock, not being able to move except for the guard who had opened the door. He rushed outside, picked up the wounded man and brought him inside. Blood was spurting from the man's leg as he continued to scream and pleaded with his eyes for someone to stop the bleeding. The guard, who brought in the injured man, had been in the Somali army and had some medical training. He took off his shirt, tore it into strips and applied a tourniquet, stemming the flow of blood. Hassan took control of the situation and told us that, if we wanted to save the man's life, we had to leave the safety of the building, and try to get him to a hospital as soon as possible. There was some urgency in Hassan's voice, even so we hesitated to move until one of the guards acted.

He lifted the injured man as gently as possible, but the pain, from even the slightest movement, caused him to scream. The wounded man was placed in the second row seat of the vehicle lying down with his head resting in the guard's lap. Hassan and another guard, riding shotgun, took their seats, while the rest of us piled up in the third row seat and the cargo bay. By that time, the shelling was directed to the northwest of our position, so there was little danger of our being injured or killed by exploding shells.

Hassan, not wanting to draw undue attention, and because of the injured man, drove at a moderate speed towards the first checkpoint. Mercifully it was deserted. There was, therefore, no need to stop, and waste precious time explaining why we were in the area. The checkpoint at the Green Line was manned, but the guards must have remembered our vehicle that had passed through less than an hour earlier. Hassan had slowed to a crawl as we came to the checkpoint and was prepared to stop, but a guard lifted the barrier and waved us through. We went directly to the United Nations Field Hospital and turned over the injured man to the medical staff. Efforts were made to stabilize him, and a few days later he was up and about and very grateful for the help he had received.

In the days that followed I kept thinking about how close I came to being blown to bits during my foray into the northern part of the city. My nights were filled with nothing else but explosions and the man who had lost his leg. It was difficult for me to shake a feeling of doom that had now become a part of my everyday life.

My wife sat and listened as I continued to relay some of the things that happened to me in Mogadishu. I could see that she wanted to interrupt my narrative, but I would not allow her to put in a word of her own. I did not want to give her a platform until I had convinced her to lay off trying to get me to travel to New York, so I continued with how I felt about UNDP. As I spoke, I kept looking at my wife to ascertain if I were getting through to her. She seemed amenable to the suggestion I had so skillfully crafted, at least in my mind, that traveling to New York was not an option for me.

My wife soon became tired of my equivocating. She countered my concerns by adding her feelings about the flight, including the comfort of traveling first class. She reminded me that the flight crew would be attentive to ensure our comfort. She also said that she had booked a flight on British Airways for that evening, and had also made arrangements with Hassan to take us to the airport. She assumed that she had gotten through to me; that I understood the risk of remaining in Nairobi when the pain in my abdomen was still to be diagnosed. Also, she tried to impress on me that any further delay would upset our children who were waiting anxiously for us in New York.

Our children knew about the ordeal and about the night when I almost passed away. They also knew about the relapse, the constant pain, and felt their mother's anxiety albeit through the telephone lines. My wife had convinced herself that I would not jeopardize my health by insisting on staying in Nairobi. But she had been wrong. That night December 23, as she was making the final preparations, I informed her that I could not, would not get on an airplane that night. Perhaps I would feel better the following day.

The next day came, and she was forced to endure the same unreasonable resistance to flying out of Nairobi that night. She understood the trauma I had endured and my reluctance to be on an aircraft, but could not empathize because the alternative was detrimental to me. It was Christmas Eve, and her hope of being home for Christmas seemed to be evaporating. Raquel felt distraught and alone in a strange place with an extremely ill husband. There were no close family members to help her contend with my recalcitrance, to share in the burden of dealing with me under such trying circumstances.

She was at the end of her tether, trying to convince me that my fear was psychological since the physical aspect of the journey did not appear to have been the problem. As a matter of fact, she reminded me; she had upgraded our travel from business to first class where the seats were more comfortable and could be converted and made up like a bed. Additionally, she added, I would be given pajamas and all the comforts of flying at night. I also liked the idea of the special foods served on those flights, although I was not the least bit interested in eating. I tried to convince myself that things were not as bad as they seemed. I told my wife that I liked the idea of passing through London, where I would be able to buy my favorite cigarettes. She immediately reminded me that smoking was out of the question, and that I had not smoked since the ordeal began. Nevertheless, I latched on to the idea of at least one pleasurable activity, and the trip did not seem to hold such terrors as they had before.

Our transport to the airport arrived at 1900 hours on Christmas Eve, more than sufficient time to catch the flight at 2300 hours. My wife realized that she had to use subterfuge, or whatever it took to get us out that night. I heard the door bell and knew that the driver had come to take us to the airport. At that moment I forgot my resolve of an hour earlier, and began to make the usual excuses why we could not travel. However, my wife had made up her mind that Christmas Eve was the day we were leaving no matter how much I protested. Her face, manner, and the way she spoke told me that this was it; I had no more say in the matter—we were leaving like it or not. I felt all of her pent up frustrations and fears as soon as I started to make excuses. She spoke even toned, not raising her voice; her calm belied her nervousness. We are leaving tonight; she had said, no excuses; no reasons no matter how plausible would be accepted.

My wife continued to relate that my life was on the line, and nothing was going to come in the way of our taking that flight, that night. She told me that she understood my fear of being cooped up on an airplane for the nine hour flight to London, the six hour layover at the airport in London, and the seven hour flight to New York. Everything had been arranged, just as before; the wheelchair on all legs of the journey and the extra assistance at check-in and aboard the aircraft—all the same I hesitated initially.

However, I saw my wife's resolve so I had nothing to say. I just motioned the driver to carry the bags to the vehicle. Raquel was stunned but did not show her surprise. True to her word, all arrangements for a smooth passage, from the check-in counter at the Nairobi Airport, security and settling in on the airplane, had been made. I was comfortable on the flight to London, and even managed to walk around the VIP lounge at Heathrow Airport. I purchased two cartons of Davidoff cigarettes, my favorite brand, and even derived some pleasure merely at the thought of lighting up. I had not smoked since my ordeal began but, all the same, I latched on to the thought.

The second leg of the journey from London to New York was pleasant enough. There was no thought of my fear of being cooped up; claustrophobia did not even enter my mind; the pain had also become a dull ache. The flight had the same effect as a sedative and, before I fell asleep, I thought that perhaps I should book a lifelong flight to keep the pain at bay.

The journey was uneventful. We arrived at JFK around 1500 hours on Christmas day. We navigated immigration and customs with ease since there were relatively few people travelling on Christmas Day. The officers on duty seemed bored and waved us through customs as if we were an inconvenience, getting in the way of more important things they could have been doing.

The day was sunny, but extremely cold with below freezing temperatures. Since my wife had arranged for a Limo to pick us up we did not have to wait in the cold for a taxi, which would have been most uncomfortable for me. I could not bear the extreme cold even though I was wearing a winter coat, hat, gloves, and a scarf. We had anticipated returning to New York during winter, so we were prepared.

The trip from JFK to our home on 90th Street and Columbus Avenue in Manhattan went well. After all the drama, we finally arrived home. Our daughters were surprised to see me in such an emaciated state. They knew I was ill, but the stark reality of how serious it was did not really sink in until they saw me. I was pale, weak and had lost about 40 pounds. Their dismay showed in their faces, but they did not comment, only furtive glances between them revealed their thoughts. They watched me as I climbed the twelve stairs, with some difficulty, to our apartment, but I assured them that I would be alright.

The apartment was festively decorated with the fresh smell of a live Christmas tree giving a special touch to the occasion. There was the smell of fresh baked cookies and other goodies that, at other times, would have teased my sense of smell. Although food was the farthest thing from my mind, the thought of edibles, other than honey, was exhilarating. It was a homecoming to be remembered by my wife because she was home. The ordeal of Nairobi seemed like something in the distant past, even though we had only left there the day before. One nightmare was over, but it was to be replaced with many more in the days and weeks that were to follow.

12

Diagnosis and Prognosis

"If you believe in God, truly believe,
Then you must get down on your hands and knees
And implore Him to save your husband."
Dr. Kevin Cahill

The prognosis indicated, rather demanded that it was a time for prayers. The kind of prayers that are offered up when all hope for recovery is gone; when only divine intervention would spell the difference between a miraculous healing and a trip to the cemetery. Dr. Kevin Cahill came to that conclusion and, in a quiet voice, told my wife that, if she believed in God, truly believed, she should get down on her hands and knees and implore Him to intercede and save my life. Medical professionals had come to the conclusion that their expertise had been stretched to their limits, and had given me some five percent chance of surviving the illness that had taken hold of me.

The doctor's words resonated with such clarity that, for the first time since the ordeal began Raquel, truly understood the gravity of the situation. She understood that my life hung in a delicate balance between life and death and that she was totally helpless at that critical time in her life. The desperation was as palpable and as real as the voices outside and within; the voices of friends and family who tried their best to comfort her, and her inner voice that was at conflict; at one time consoling and almost simultaneously telling her that I was going to die.

Two weeks before consulting with Dr. Kevin Cahill, Raquel and I had come to New York from Nairobi. Raquel had consulted with the UN Medical Service soon after our arrival in New York in December 1993. She was sure that they would have been able to give us valuable information on my condition and make a recommendation for a Tropical Disease Specialist. We were directed to consult with a specialist at New York Hospital.

I had my first appointment with the doctor during the first week of January 1994 and, after examining me, without the added support of a blood test, he concluded that there was no evidence of typhoid. With obvious consternation in her voice, Raquel wanted to know what the diagnosis was if typhoid had been ruled out. The doctor responded confidently that I did not have red spots on my stomach, so I did not have or could not have had typhoid fever.

The confidence the doctor felt was not shared by either of us particularly when he announced that he would be away for two weeks. In the meantime, his colleague would attend to me as required. He dismissed my concern about the constant pain I was experiencing and recommended that I should stop taking the anti-biotic, Amoxicillin, immediately. According to him, the drug was the main reason for my malaise and lack of appetite. The pain was to be treated with a prescription strength pain killer, and if it got worse the doctor, who was standing in, would make an appropriate recommendation.

Raquel and I stepped out of the doctor's office feeling worse than when we left home that morning. It was not that the disease had progressed any further during the course of the day. Despair had set in since, contrary to what we had expected, no resolution was even hinted at during my consultation with the Tropical Disease Specialist.

This was the conundrum; this was the problem that caused the onset of depression a few days later that threatened to undermine our hope for a cure when we came to New York. Maybe the loss of hope caused some level of psychosis that in turn exacerbated my illness.

Within a few days after consultation with the Tropical Disease Specialist, I took a turn for the worse. The pain became unbearable without any letup day and night and night and day into endless days and nights. What little food I could stomach before became an added burden on an already overburdened body. A body racked with pain and a mind that could hardly cope with the lack of a definitive diagnosis.

Maybe the doctors in Nairobi were wrong; maybe I had contracted some other unknown, untreatable disease that had invaded my body. A disease that was slowly, but surely, choking the life out of me. In my weakened state, I often hallucinated and dreamed dreams that only a crazed mind could envisage. I thought of my body as a place where combatants were continually at war. I knew that the bad guys in this fight were winning because I grew weaker and weaker as one day melded into the next.

I was totally dependent on my wife who was at my side constantly. She talked to me with compassion trying to assure me that she understood what I was going through. Her strength and clear decisive action brought me through each day as she figured out our next move. It was during a time of deep contemplation on what we should do next that she decided the doctor I was seeing was totally useless. She felt that I should consult with another Tropical Disease Specialist, Dr. Kevin Cahill, who was on the list the UN Medical Service had given her.

"First thing tomorrow morning we will consult with Dr. Cahill. We'll go to his office and try to see him on an emergency basis since

I do not want to waste time waiting for an appointment." Raquel's words were soothing, but the anxiety in her voice was not lost on me.

"I am glad you made that decision," I responded.

That night the dreams returned; they were of impending disaster except the dreams were not actually dreams, but were a vivid kaleidoscope of events in my past that had threatened my life. The events in which I played a leading role could not be dreams. For them to be dreams, I would have had to be asleep. I did not think that I had even dozed off; I remembered the pain, the twisting and turning to find a comfortable spot that would, at least, ease the pain. Instead, in my mind, I had lain awake all through the night until the first rays of the sun, announcing that another day had begun, seeped through the curtains of our bedroom window.

Without any prompting one from the other, both of us rose in unison and started to prepare for the ordeal that would ensue. The trip to the doctor's office was going to be difficult because even the walk from our bedroom to the living room, just a few stairs down, zapped my strength.

Dr. Cahill's first reaction upon laying eyes on me was a question that was pregnant with foreboding.

"Why are you not in a hospital, Mr. Dillett? You are obviously in extreme pain and practically comatose." Dr. Cahill asked.

"That's the reason for our being here doctor," Raquel responded. "The UN Medical Service had directed us to a doctor at New York Hospital but, a few days ago, he left us in the care of one of his colleague. I was not satisfied with his demeanor towards my husband, so I made the decision last night to consult you today on an emergency basis. My husband was diagnosed with typhoid fever in Nairobi over eight weeks ago and was treated in the Nairobi Hospital, but his condition worsened. That was the reason for coming to New York. According to the first doctor we saw at New

York Hospital, my husband was misdiagnosed because there was no evidence of his having contracted typhoid fever, despite the report from the doctor in Nairobi."

"What was his diagnosis then?" asked Dr. Cahill.

I spoke, for the first time since entering the room, extremely slowly my words punctuated with bouts of heavy breathing. But I spoke clearly, so that my every word could be understood the first time because I did not think I had the energy to repeat myself

"The doctor did not know, but he was certain it could not have been typhoid fever because a major symptom, present in all typhoid cases, did not manifest itself in me."

"And what was that?" Dr. Cahill asked

"I did not have or are there now red spots on my abdomen." I replied.

Dr. Cahill smiled but did not respond. He proceeded with his examination, drew blood and said, with a mischievous smile on his face,

"You are a black man. Therefore red spots would not show through your dark skin. Red spots are reserved for people with fair to white skin where the red can be seen quite easily."

The moment of levity passed. It was replaced with deep concern as Dr. Cahill's observed my demeanor, my discomfort, my every twist and turn in an effort to find a comfortable position where the pain was less evident.

"I am sure that it was typhoid and that some damage has been done to your abdominal aorta," Dr. Cahill said. "I came to this conclusion from the Nairobi medical report, the description of the relapse, Raquel's excellent notes and the abdominal pain."

Dr. Cahill was very concerned about the pain I described; he suspected the presence of an aneurysm but he said nothing at that time. He ordered a CT-scan that was to be done just a few doors down the street from his office. It was a painful process for me just to walk from Dr. Cahill's office to the Center for the CT-scan; it required super human effort to set one foot in front of the other. Notwithstanding the pain, the task was accomplished with the patient assistance and encouragement of Raquel.

The Radiologist was a kind and gentle man and spoke softly as he prepared me for the CT-scan. Halfway into the procedure he confirmed the presence of an abdominal aneurysm that appeared to be on the verge of rupturing. After consulting with Dr. Cahill on the phone, an ambulance was called and I was whisked to Lenox Hill Hospital for an emergency operation.

Dr. Ahmed Maher and his team of vascular specialists were waiting at the landing bay of the Emergency Room as the ambulance pulled up. They immediately took me into their charge and commenced prepping me for emergency surgery. Dr. Cahill had contacted Dr. Ahmed earlier with a special favor to take my case although it was an inopportune time for Dr. Ahmed.

His father-in-law had passed away a few days earlier and he had assigned all his cases to another vascular surgeon at Lenox Hill. But Dr. Cahill wanted to ensure that I received the best treatment so he petitioned Dr. Ahmed to take charge. The team sprang into action under Dr. Ahmed watchful eye; he examined the CT-scan film closely and confirmed that there was no time to lose, if the aneurysm ruptured there would have been nothing anyone could do to save my life even if I were on the operating table. So he worked in haste, but with attention to details that is typical of a great doctor and surgeon.

The beehive of activity in the room heightened the psychological tension. I was poignantly aware of every movement in the room, the eyes that were focused on me, all tinged with sorrow and compassion. I felt a tender but nervous hand on my penis as an Intern tried to catheterize me. She was so nervous she kept dropping the tube in her effort to get it up the urethra and into my bladder. There was no pain in the process but the actions of the Intern were a distraction as I tried to cope with the reality of the moment and what was to come when I was on the operating table. Dr. Ahmed was aware of the Intern's dilemma so he instructed her to wait until I was under anesthesia to complete her task.

Dr. Ahmed did not have the time to explain the procedure to me. Actually it was not that there was not sufficient time but the fact that I could not understand what was happening to me. I could not follow any trend of thought or explanations. Words did not matter one iota to me; what mattered was the unrelenting pain; what mattered was that I had not slept, really slept for longer than I cared to remember. I was so tired that I had asked my wife to take me home to rest for a while even as the ambulance was waiting to take me to the hospital.

The inability to fathom the dire situation was not new. The fever must have fried my brain or had done something to alter my thought process, or my ability to absorb and act on complicated issues. Reality had not crept in so Dr. Ahmed's explanation of what had to be done, in an attempt to save my life, did not register with me. This was not lost on both Dr. Ahmed and Dr. Cahill and so all explanations of procedures and permission to perform them were entrusted to my wife. That was Nairobi all over again.

"Dr. Cahill and I will do all in our power to save your husband's life," Dr. Ahmed told Raquel. "However we must be honest with you and prepare you for the worse. There is extensive damage to your husband's abdominal aorta. It is so extensive and the aorta so inflamed that we fear it might rupture at any time."

Dr. Ahmed continued quietly being careful to keep me from hearing what was being said:

"This operation may very well be exploratory because we will only know the extent of the damage when we physically examine the aorta."

One of Dr. Ahmed's assistants came up to him and whispered something in his ear that Raquel could not hear. She suspected that it had to do with some new discovery that would add to an already bad situation. But no new information was forthcoming. Dr. Ahmed merely told Raquel to say goodbye to me as they were ready to proceed. He also told her, in a soft voice, that her goodbye might be her last because of the bleak prognosis on the result of the operation. It was at this point that Raquel suddenly slumped and would have fallen to the floor if Dr. Cahill have not caught her and gently held her until she managed to steady herself.

Try as she might Raquel could not hide her despair as she approached the hospital gurney where I lay, waiting to be wheeled into the Operating Room. I had watched her intently as she approached and asked why she was crying. She did not want me to know the gravity of the situation, though she suspected that I knew, so she lied and said that she had caught a cold. The tears were her eyes watering uncontrollably and the sobbing her body's way of fighting off the cold. Her explanation made no sense at all but mercifully, she was spared having to explain the unexplainable because at the very point, when I was about to question her, an orderly came and took me away. And so my wife was left with her thoughts that were jumbled and filled with foreboding.

What else could she have done? She had called family and friends and had implored them to pray and to keep a vigil for her beloved. The Head Nurse, knowing the gravity of the situation, and in an attempt to ease her burden, had given Raquel permission to use her office as her command center and the telephone was at her disposal. She could call anywhere in the world to let family and friends know how critical the situation was with me. The children had been informed about my health that had deteriorated to such an extent that the doctors were not holding out much hope for my recovery.

Alex, the eldest from a previous marriage, had left his home in Belize and tried to enter the USA, clandestinely, from Mexico. He could not fathom the circumstance surrounding my health, or lack thereof. How could his father have become so sick in so short a space of time? The inevitability of death and the passage from the Book of Common Prayer "In the midst of life we are in death," did not have meaning for him as he pondered that he might not see his father alive again.

Jennifer, the first child with Raquel, had skipped classes at New York University and had met her mother in the Emergency Room. She kept plying the staff with questions about her father's condition that they could not answer.

Melanie, the youngest of the brood, was told that her father had been taken to the hospital for an emergency operation. Without asking the whys and wherefores, she had left her campus at Spelman College in Atlanta and had flown to New York City on the first available flight.

As Raquel sat in the hospital waiting room with Jennifer, her parents and a few close friends she began second guessing herself about the course of action she had taken since we had arrived in New York. As a matter of fact she wondered whether or not she had done all that was in her power, while we were in Nairobi, to ensure that I received the best care.

"The Lord will keep your husband," she heard someone say.

Raquel turned to see the Hospital Chaplain, Ann Campbell, sitting next to her. She was not even aware of the Chaplain's presence but felt a comforting sense of relief in her words. Raquel knew that everything was in God's hands; she knew that the doctors were skilled in their chosen fields. Dr. Cahill, the Tropical Disease Specialist and Dr. Maher Ahmed the Vascular Surgeon whose expertise was to be tested to its fullest extent before the day was done.

Raquel tried to remember exactly what Dr. Cahill had told her. His words had brought some comfort to her because, for the first time in her life, she heard a doctor calling on the name of the Lord. There was solace also, because the doctor was doing so on my behalf. The doctors she knew were men of science; men who subscribed to the big bang theory, not some God who called everything into existence. Raquel thought that there really was no difference between the world coming together by chance, and it being created by a Supernatural Being. It was all a matter of philosophy, what one chose to believe.

"Why these views of creation and the big bang theory at this time?" She wondered to herself. "Why am I trying to reconcile my thoughts and beliefs to fit into this mode of thinking or philosophy? Am I hedging my bet just in case and placing myself in a positive frame of mind so that God would look kindly on my husband?"

Raquel estimated that some three hours had passed since I was wheeled into the Operating room. That was a fleeting thought as she continued to talk to herself about God and creation and wondering, at the same time, if the doctors were still battling to save my life. Just as those thoughts were going through her mind, she became aware of some movement at the entrance to the waiting room. She shifted her gaze to the door as Melanie came rushing into the room.

Melanie hustled in her eyes scanning the faces of each person sitting there until they locked with her mother's. She hurried over, not noticing the other members of the family who were also waiting patiently for word from the Operating Room. She stumbled into her mother's arms scarcely able to contain the emotions that were swirling within her from the time she received word that I had to undergo emergency surgery. The sobs came, controlled at first, then the flood gates opened and she cried salty tears rolling down her cheeks. The sudden turn in her dad's illness had not sunken in until that very moment.

"I knew that Dad was sick, considering how ghastly he looked when you guys returned from Nairobi, but this emergency surgery took me by surprise." Melanie was able to get her words out in between sobs.

"It's alright," her mother told her. "But it is not quite time for tears yet. I am hopeful that time is a long way off. Now it is time to pray and ask the Lord to be with the Surgeon and his assistants as they try to save your father's life."

As Raquel hugged Melanie and tried to comfort her, Jennifer came up and placed her arms around her sister and her mother. She too had commenced crying again taking her cue from her sister. As they stood there, Raquel filled Melanie in on what had transpired so far. She told her that her dad was, at that very moment, undergoing the operation and they were all waiting for the doctor to emerge from the Operating Room.

About an hour later Dr. Ahmed came into the room and, taking Raquel aside, told her in whispered tones that the extent of the damage to my aorta was much more extensive than had been originally envisaged. Dr. Ahmed had therefore aborted the operation in order to consult with other specialists at Lenox Hill and other major hospitals in the area to determine the best course of action.

"The aneurysm did not rupture, but a section of your husband's abdominal aorta is damaged beyond repair." Dr. Ahmed told Raquel. "We will try to replace the damaged area with a graft. We are not sure how this will work because of the location of the damage, but we will enlist the help of specialists in this field."

Raquel was speechless as she listened to Dr. Ahmed's report. However she forced herself to focus on what was being relayed to her. She wanted to ask questions but could not quite form the words; she could not even think lucidly enough to form coherent thoughts. Thoughts when translated into words would convey her innermost fear, her fear that I was going to die. She told herself that she would not think of death because the very thought might induce dreaded Death to take hold of me and whisk me away.

"There are some technical details that I would like to discuss with you," Dr. Ahmed told Raquel. "Perhaps we should go to my office where we can speak in private."

The suggestion was acceptable since Raquel did not want to have a public hearing on my condition. Someone had, earlier that day, berated her for not taking action soon enough. The implication was that if she had acted sooner, I would not be in such a horrible state. That was the reason for her earlier reflection on steps she had taken when I became ill. As she accompanied Dr. Ahmed to his office, walking like someone in a trance, her mind strayed to Nairobi once more, and the difficult time she had, even as I was apparently getting better. One thing was for sure, she had done all in her power to make sure that I received the best treatment. She resolved that she would not allow anyone to tell her anything to the contrary in future.

"You may sit down Mrs. Dillett," Dr. Ahmed told her.

Raquel turned and was startled at her surroundings. She had walked the corridors of the hospital with Dr. Ahmed in a day dream until his words brought her back to the present.

"Dr. Cahill will join us in a few minutes." Dr. Ahmed announced. "At that time, we will explain what we found and what we plan to do. Would you like some coffee or tea while we wait?"

"Yes thanks, coffee will do," Raquel replied.

A few minutes after coffee was served, Dr. Cahill walked into the room and suggested that Dr. Ahmed start the briefing. Dr. Ahmed went to great lengths to describe what had happened commencing with the CT-scan. The scan had shown an unclear picture of the aorta. The ill-defined picture was due to a mass or phlegm that covered the aorta starting from the superior mesenteric artery to below the renal arteries. Below the mass, a lemon size aneurysm was apparent that stopped short of the bifurcation, that is, the point where the aorta dissected into two veins that stretch down into the legs.

Dr. Ahmed talked about entering the abdominal cavity by making a mid-line incision extending from just below the sternum to the pubis. It was apparent that there was not only the aneurysm that appeared to be on the verge of rupturing, but also the aorta was obscured by an infection. As Dr. Ahmed spoke, Raquel became lost in the details and found herself dwelling so long on each word that she could not follow the thread of the brief. She did not want to interrupt the doctor, but it became necessary to do just that since the brief was losing its intent.

About the same time she was contemplating her course of action, Dr. Ahmed also became aware that he was not getting through to Raquel because of going into the technical details. Such details that the lay person would have a hard time to follow. Dr. Ahmed explained that there was extensive damage to my aorta. The condition was known as an infected abdominal aortic aneurysm (IAAA). There was an area of the aorta that was so badly degraded that it would not hold sutures.

It was therefore pointless to continue so the operation was aborted until a suitable graft could be found to repair my aorta. Dr. Ahmed then told Raquel that he had to remove my spleen that had been irreparably damaged during the exploratory surgery. He also said that he had removed my gall bladder as a precaution against possible future infection. Typhoid had a nasty habit of hiding in the gall bladder and while I would be typhoid free I could become a carrier and infect other people.

"Do you know the story of Typhoid Mary who, in 1907 in New York, became the first know carrier of typhoid bacilli and, although she was health, she had infested a number of people with the bacteria?" Dr. Ahmed had asked.

"Yes," Raquel responded.

"Then there is no need to go into the details of why I thought it necessary to remove the gall bladder," Dr. Ahmed said.

My case was the first that presented so many technical difficulties for Dr. Ahmed. In fact he felt something of a reprieve in having to abort the operation. He was at a loss how to continue when he was faced with such extensive damage. He did not, of course, share those thoughts with Raquel. He and Dr. Cahill would have to mull over their course of action including consulting with doctors in other well-known institutions in the country and abroad.

In the meantime he spoke about their preparation for the second operation that was to take place within the next few days. He told Raquel that I was being sent to the ICU and should be awake in about one hour. An angiogram of the aorta was being arranged for the next day. Dr. Ahmed paused again being aware that he had lost Raquel once more when he mentioned the word "angiogram". It was important for Raquel to understand all the procedures not necessarily in detail, but to have an idea of the difficulties involved in treating me.

Raquel would have preferred, at this point, to be blissfully ignorant of the details. She did not even want to tax her brain with all the technical jargon, no matter how brief the explanations were. She only wanted to hear of a positive result. She was even prepared, no rather needed, to get some good news even if the news were not entirely accurate. She just wanted some respite from the months of stress she had been experiencing. She just wanted to be able to postpone the inevitable bad news that she was sure was coming somewhere down the road. She realized though that she had to listen and give her full attention to what was being said.

So she picked up on the term "angiogram" and asked for an explanation. The mortality rate associated with abdominal aortic aneurysms was quite high; and in order to improve on the patient's chance of survival, it was necessary to do a preoperative evaluation. A dye is injected in the aorta and x-rays are taken to map the damaged section of the aorta. Dr. Ahmed would then be in a better position to determine the best course of action during the upcoming operation which was scheduled for January 19.

The date resonated with Raquel. She was born on January 18. She wondered how she would spend her 44th birthday knowing that the next day was going to be one of the most challenging in her life. Dr. Ahmed glanced at Raquel and decided that he should conclude the briefing at that point. But before doing so he promised to discuss the operation after the angiogram was done. Raquel gratefully accepted the reprieve, and after thanking both doctors for taking her husband's case, she left and headed for the Waiting Room. She knew the news was not as good as she had hoped, but what Dr. Ahmed had told her was all she had.

Everyone was waiting anxiously for word on my condition. Raquel gathered everyone in a corner of the room and repeated what Dr. Ahmed had told her. No one spoke, no questions were asked as Raquel tried to bring everyone up to speed on my situation. It was as if each person understood instinctively that whatever she said was all the information she had to give. She told them that I was doing well under the circumstances, was resting in the ICU and would undergo a more extensive operation within a few days.

That night Raquel called her sister in Irvine, California and my sister in Miami. She provided details on how I was doing, and promised to update them as things progressed. Both assured her that they were coming to New York to stand in solidarity with her during those critical times. She was grateful for their support particularly when they told her they were with her, not only in spirit, but they would also be with her physically. Thoughts of the support she had received from her family, my family and some friends warmed her heart. She could not, however, escape the nagging thoughts that occupied her every waking moment when she was not engaged in attending to those around her. While I was in good hands, she did not consider that to be amnesty from worrying about my welfare. So she worried and kept going over the events in Nairobi and what had happened since we arrived in New York. There were other things that occupied her mind, the most important of which was the upcoming angiogram.

The Sunday before the operation January 16, most family members, close friends and a number of my colleagues from the UN crowded into the ICU at various times during the day. Word had got out that the possibility of my surviving the operation was less than slim, so they all came to say goodbye. No one said the word "goodbye", of course. They just stood, some crying softly as they looked at me with genuine sorrow in their countenances. There were whispered prayers, petitions made to the Almighty for a successful outcome of the operation on January 19, though there was little chance that I would pull through. The prayers and display of subdued emotions had a calming effect on me. I knew the gravity of the situation; that I could die on the Operating Table and yet, for some unfathomable reason, I did not call on the name of the Lord.

ANTHONY DILLET

13

The Operation

*"Then he said, This is what I'll do.
I will tear down my barns and build bigger ones,
and there I will store my surplus grain."*
Luke 12:18

I was extremely cold as I waited for the attendant to take me to the X-ray room. Raquel could see that I was shivering uncontrollably, my teeth chattering so loudly that it practically drowned out the sounds of the beeps from the intravenous infusion pumps that kept me fed and hydrated. I was brought directly to the ICU after the first operation, and remained wide awake most of the time, particularly at nights when I should have been sleeping. There was no relief from the unrelenting pain that seemed to be getting worse.

Dr. Ahmed had left strict instructions that I was not to be given any sedatives. He wanted me to be alert because of the potential that the aneurysm might rupture. Being sedated would not allow me to feel any change in the intensity of the pain and that could be fatal. Dr. Ahmed explained that the slightest increase in the pain was to be reported to him immediately since that could have signaled that the aneurysm had ruptured or was about to rupture. In that event he would have had to operate immediately, without the benefit of the angiogram and additional expertise he hoped to have by the time of the operation.

Raquel had alerted the nurse to my discomfort. At first one blanket was used and when that did not help then two and eventually three blankets covered my emaciated frame. Just as I was warming up the attendant came and took me for the angiogram. Raquel accompanied me, holding my hand. She knew instinctively, and from the look in my eyes that fear of the procedure had crept into my psyche. She stayed with me and went as far as she could go, all the while speaking to me, consoling and assuring me that all would be well. I had squeezed her hand and smiled up at her as I was wheeled away. Raquel felt a sense of comfort at my reaction to her presence and what she had said. She also felt a supernatural presence signaling that we were not alone and, at that time, a glimmer of hope began to well up inside her.

The cold, stark and impersonal ambiance of the X-ray room unnerved me as the Radiologist prepared me for the angiogram. The incision in my groin area did not bother me. I felt nothing as the catheter went up the aorta dispensing some type of contract dye to make the blood vessels opaque. Dr. Ahmed had explained that as the dye is injected, a series of x-ray images would be taken to map the damaged section of the aorta and blood flow in the arteries. The procedure was routine but, like any invasive medical procedure, things could go wrong.

I was confident that I would come through unscathed, except for the excessive exposure to radiation that was inevitable. That bothered me tremendously and, as the camera snapped away, I was sure that the metal under the flimsy pad beneath me was getting progressively hotter each time a picture was taken. It seemed to me that I had lain there for hours when, in fact, the whole procedure had only lasted for about half an hour. I had to remain where I was, although it was uncomfortable, until the Radiologist reviewed the x-rays to ensure that the images were adequate.

The intercom between the room where I waited and the Radiologist station was open. They must have thought that I was asleep or had simply forgotten to close the window. That was how I heard a hushed conversation between the Radiologist and his assistant about what the angiogram revealed. The images confirmed the extent of the damage to my aorta. They showed the location of the aneurysm and the difficulties the doctor was going to have in repairing it. In addition, another diagnosis was made. The left renal artery was infected with the same phlegm like matter that had invaded my aorta.

I heard, but the import of the discovery did not penetrate my already overburdened brain. I decided that I was powerless to do anything about the information I had overheard. I allowed my mind to drift and was relieved to fall asleep. I neither heard when the all clear was given, nor did I feel the movement of the gurney as I was wheeled back to the ICU. I had a fleeting recollection of seeing Raquel as I slipped off into blissful sleep that had been sporadic from the time my ordeal began.

I slept and dreamed about better days. As a matter of fact, the dreams centered on being well; about plans to roam the world with my wife, taking assignments that suited us until it was time for retirement. It occurred to me in my reverie that I had forgotten what was important in our lives. I was preoccupied with what we were going to do in the aftermath of my run-in with the Rangers, and my disappointment with UNDP. The "we" and what "we" were going to do took precedence over everything else. In my dream I became poignantly aware of a specific parable in the Bible and, while I could not remember the chapter and verse at the time, I remembered the story quite well.

I dreamt about the man who had a bountiful harvest. He did not have sufficient space in his barns to store the harvest, so he made a plan what *he* was going to do. *He* would tear down the old barns and build bigger ones and store all *his* goods. *He* said to himself that *he* had much goods laid up for the future. *He* would take *his* ease and eat, drink and be merry. But God had other plans for him and he found out soon enough that his plans were futile, that his life was not his own.

I awoke from my sleep and, for a few moments, could not figure out where I was. The stark white room, the tubes attached to my body and the beep, beep of machines were disconcerting. Then I remembered where I was. I felt a deep sense of disappointment that my wife and I were not on our way to some exotic place. Instead, I was laid up in a hospital bed waiting for an operation that would determine whether I lived or died.

Live or die brought back memory of my dream, the parable, and the fate of the man who had forgotten his purpose in life. The man who made *his* plans based on *his* success. At that point, I saw myself standing precisely where that man stood in his arrogance about what he had achieved. I realized that I had paid no attention to my spiritual life, only what would satisfy my physical needs. I thought that I was not going to build anything and that being ill was meant to show me that I was not in control. It showed me that I was as vulnerable as any human being to the vicissitudes of life, that I knew nothing of tomorrow and that my plans were futile.

Even as those thoughts were coursing through my mind, it did not occur to me to bargain with God for my life, though the next day might very well be my last on this earth. The thought never occurred to me to have a conversation with my Maker, just in case I did not come out of the Operating Room alive. My life was slipping away, but today was still in my mind, not what tomorrow might bring.

Although I was wide awake my eyes were closed as I reminisced over what was, and possibly, what was to come. I was not aware that Raquel was in the room watching me closely, feeling a sense of relief that I had, at long last, fallen asleep. She was drained because she was on constant alert, watching me even when there were professionals around who took care of my every need. She had dozed off, and the book she was reading fell out of her hand. She awoke when the book hit the floor with a thud that was scarcely audible, but was loud enough to alert me that someone was in the room.

I opened my eyes and saw Raquel trying to retrieve the book from off the floor. I had greeted her with a bright:

"Hi there."

She was a little sad at having awakened me, but I assured her that, although my eyes were closed, I had been wide awake for at least fifteen minutes. We then talked about the angiogram and the fact that Dr. Ahmed had not contacted either one of us about the results. I related the conversation I had overheard about the findings of the angiogram. Both of us had our individual views as to what was more devastating than what we had already been told—the infection that encompassed my aorta or the infection that was encroaching on my left renal artery—but neither of us wanted to discussed the challenges posed by the additional information that was brought to our attention.

Once again the future was bleak, and more bad news could wait. That evening Dr. Ahmed and two of his assistants came to the ICU, somber expressions on their faces. It was as if the news they were about to impart were a death sentence. Their countenances conveyed a terrible reality, that there existed little hope for a successful outcome. They did not intend to show such negativity, but the information they had been mulling over during the past 10 or so hours was not encouraging. It was also not going to be easy to describe the process they had devised to repair my aorta.

"I am not in any frame of mind to take bad news graciously," I said to Dr. Ahmed with a measure of humor in my voice.

Dr. Ahmed smiled wryly, a touch of sadness in his voice as he tried to level with us about the road ahead. He went to great lengths to describe the outcome of the angiogram, and illustrated the gravity of the situation by using the actual diagrams and conclusions of the Radiologist. There was no easy way to get across what they all knew. It was even more difficult for Dr. Ahmed to explain what he did not know, and how he planned to bridge the gap when he came across something they did not anticipate.

Dr. Ahmed and his team had spent countless hours on the phone with every renowned medical institution in the country and in England. They were searching for information on vascular degeneration caused by typhoid fever. They had spoken to medical experts at the Mayo Clinic, the Center for Disease Control, New York Columbia Presbyterian Hospital, the University College Hospital in London, and a number of other institutions. Not one of those places had any expertise in dealing with the type of damage that presented itself in my case. So Dr. Ahmed and his team had to devise their own strategies in their efforts to save my life.

We did not have to wait long for Dr. Ahmed to brief us on the other difficulties the angiogram had revealed. The additional problems presented were the infected left renal artery and the poor aortic wall around it. In order to repair the aorta, the left renal artery would have to be removed with the kidney intact. The service of a Nephrologist was essential to keep the kidney functioning until it could be reattached after the aorta was repaired.

The procedure was quite risky and could affect the right kidney also. In the event both kidneys failed to function after the operation, I would be on dialysis until I could have a kidney transplant. With respect to the spine, Dr. Ahmed said he would be required to work close to the thoracic section of my spine. Any misstep could render me paralyzed from the waist down. Unchartered territory, Dr. Ahmed, had called the operation, but he assured us that he and his colleagues were going to use their combined expertise to have a successful outcome.

The night before the operation Raquel stayed in the ICU with me though the head nurse told her it was against the rules. Raquel paid no attention to her and with the help of the nurse's assistant, made the easy chair into a bed. It was uncomfortable as was expected, but she wanted to be near me for what could very well be our last night together. There was no conversation between us only silence, and the occasional wan smile, each conveying our innermost feelings. Tomorrow would bring what it may, but that night we were together.

We both slept fitfully, not giving much thought about the morrow, and the operation that Dr. Ahmed had said would last for about ten hours. There was no thought of death. We did not think about the day after tomorrow. We just waited for the hands on the clock to move from one hour to the next, waiting for 0500 hours when the attendants were scheduled to take me to the Operating Room. And, after what seemed like an eternity, the attendants came.

There was no one in the corridors except for the Hospital Chaplain who seemed to have stood vigil over my room, lifting me up in prayers. She had arrived at the ICU around 0300 hours and had looked in on me. She had observed Raquel and me sleeping fitfully. Today was going to be a tough one for both of them, the Chaplain thought, so she had pulled up a chair and sat by the door in quiet meditation. Ann Campbell had met us on the first day when I was admitted to the hospital. She had taken an immediate liking to Raquel, a woman in desperate straits because her husband was gravely ill.

In the days following their first encounter, Pastor Ann had observed Raquel and the family dynamics as they supported each other. The Pastor thought about the interaction of other families as they went through similar situations. In all cases except this one, there was some level of detachment among family members. Tears and wailing at times, but not the same cohesiveness and caring she had seen in Raquel's family. The Pastor was intrigued and decided to learn more about the family when the opportunity presented itself.

As Pastor Ann waited to accompany me to the Operating Room, she spoke with Raquel briefly, quietly to let her know that she was praying for her, as well. Raquel had smiled as she embraced Pastor Ann, and thanked her for the comfort and the encouragement she had provided to her and her family. There was something genuinely authentic about Pastor Ann. She was not merely doing a job when she spoke with her hospital parishioners. She empathized with them, and her spirit actually soared when she was instrumental in bringing someone to the Lord. She felt in tune with Raquel as they accompanied me to the Operating Room. The Pastor sensed Raquel's pain, her anxiety about the future. People often talked about the future in terms of weeks or months or years. But today, Ann thought, this lovely woman was measuring her future in terms of hours.

They reached the Operating Room just as Dr. Ahmed and his team arrived. Raquel said her goodbyes to me wishing that she could be in the Operating Room to see first-hand what was going on. She knew that was not possible, not only because hospital policy precluded her from being in there, but because she knew she was incapable of witnessing anything so gruesome. It took all her will power to hear what had to be done to repair my aorta, let alone observe the procedures. Before being wheeled into the Operating Room, Pastor Ann prayed with me asking for God's intervention.

"Nevertheless," she concluded her intercessory prayer, "let Your will be done."

The Pastor was not sure that I had heard a word she had said. She told me a few days later that I seemed preoccupied with my own thoughts as if I would have preferred to be somewhere else; not waiting for a life changing operation or one that would end my life. Then the attendants took me away, and for a few minutes Pastor Ann stood there absorbed with her own thoughts. She felt she had failed in trying to get me centered on spiritual things, like God's everlasting love instead of what was ahead in the Operating Room.

Raquel was preoccupied but had seen that Pastor Ann was deep in contemplation as if she had lost time, and was not aware of her environment. But that was not the case at all as she later explained to Raquel. She was actually praying for me and my doctors through the difficulties that lay ahead. She felt in her innermost self that, even with the dire circumstances, all would be well in the end. Raquel had waited for Pastor Ann although she wanted to rush to the Waiting Room where, she was sure; her children and other members of the family were waiting. Just as she was debating whether or not she should leave, the Pastor turned, smiled at her and without saying a word both started to walk to the Waiting Room.

No one was there when they arrived, so they sat in silence. The operation was scheduled to begin at 0700 hours. It was now a few minutes to the hour, and Raquel wondered why no one, at least her children, had arrived. Just then Jenni and Melanie walked into the room followed by Raquel's father, her mother, her sister and my sister. No one spoke as they sat down for the long wait. Melanie and Jenni sat next to their mother, each with an arm around her. My sister handed Raquel some coffee and a bun she had made.

"I am sure you have not eaten anything. This is going to be a long day, and you need to keep up your strength," my sister had said.

Raquel thanked her for her thoughtfulness, and began to nibble at the food absentmindedly. She was grateful to her sister-in-law for her support from the time she learned of my illness. She had told Raquel that she knew she had done all in her power to get me the help I needed. That statement was most comforting.

Raquel looked at the clock and saw that just over one hour had elapsed since the operation began. It was pointless to follow the clock, she thought, but all the same she was powerless to do anything about her anxiety because five minutes later she was looking at the clock again. The best thing she thought was to engage those around her in conversation, preferably conversation that would lift the somber mood in the room. She remembered an incident in Angola that made her smile even after so many years.

We were assigned to Angola in 1982, and I arrived in Luanda, the capital city around June of that year. Raquel and the girls joined me a few months later after spending some time with her sister and her sister's family in Irvine, California.

Luanda was a beautiful city, in many ways a replica of Lisbon, Portugal. The Portuguese had made Luanda home; so much so that most professionals, blue collar workers, drivers, technicians, you name it had been brought in from Portugal, Sao Tome and Cape Verde.

Soon after arriving in Luanda, Raquel was stopped by a traffic cop because, according to him, she was going over the speed limit. She had pretended she could not speak Portuguese, though she was fairly proficient in the language. There was a back and forth between them.

"Por favor, su licenca," (Your license, please) the cop had demanded.

"I do not understand," she had responded.

The cop finally remembered, perhaps his only English word. "License."

Raquel had produced her driver's license she had obtained when we lived in Jamaica. As soon as the cop saw the word "Jamaica" he became quite excited and asked Raquel if she knew Bob Marley (in Portuguese of course), to which she had responded:

"Si" (yes).

The cop, in his excitement at meeting someone who knew Bob Marley, forgot that Raquel had said she not did understand Portuguese; gave her back her license, stepped back, and waved her on.

Raquel had shared her experience with those around her and, for a few minutes, there was some cheerfulness in the room. Someone even started to hum "War" a popular Bob Marley song. However, the mood did not last for long, when they remembered why they were in the Waiting Room. Once more the clock became the center of Raquel's universe as she waited and waited for news about what was going on in the Operating Room.

As the hours passed and she became more preoccupied with what was happening to me, Raquel thought that perhaps no news was good news. She could not help wringing her hands, and, at times a low moan escaped her lips. Melanie had been looking at her mother intently, emotions welling up in her also, and, in that frame of mind, she was moved to write:

God's Will

"My Baby, my sweet Baby". Clasped hands
Salty Teardrops

Caressing, comforting, consoling
"My Baby, my sweet Baby".
Whispers of words
Hope and Strength
Warm sweaty hands
Grasping for support, comfort,
Consolidation, hope, strength
"God, He will take care of him, either way".
Touch, squeeze, sigh
"I know"
Eyes swollen, searching
Thinking, remembering
Life or death

Melanie's thoughts, expressed in the poem, had captured the mood in the room. She had actually read her mother's mind, her innermost thoughts as she watched her closely. Raquel had read the poem shortly after it was written, and she thought how intuitive of her daughter to have seized upon how she felt.

She had taken comfort in the words of the poem. She was particularly taken with the part that spoke about God taking care of her husband "either way". She felt contentment in those words because, by faith, she knew she would see her husband again if it were God's will to take him home that day. And, if he were to live, then there would be a celebration that would top all celebrations they had in the past. "Either way", tears had well up in her eyes as she laid her head on Melanie's shoulder.

About four hours into the operation, one of Dr. Ahmed's assistants came into the Waiting Room and walked directly to Raquel. The first thought that came to her mind was that it was too early; the operation could not have ended so soon. Something must have gone wrong. She had started to panic when she considered that Dr. Ahmed would have been the bearer of bad news, not the assistant. She also saw a smile on the assistant's face, and concluded that her presence was to deliver an update on the proceedings.

Her assumption was correct as the assistant embraced her and told her that all was going according to plan. The most difficult part of the operation was yet to come, such as the removal of the left renal artery and repair of the damaged part of the aorta. The assistant had related how Dr. Ahmed, after examining the aorta closely, remarked that he was going to become a seamstress because he had to fashion the graft to fit the damaged part of my aorta. The assistant thought that it was strange for Dr. Ahmed to refer to himself as a seamstress instead of a tailor. Perhaps that was due to the fact that Dr. Ahmed, a Palestinian, did not know that the male counterpart for seamstress was tailor. In any case, he had injected some humor in a serious atmosphere.

The brief then centered on the operation and a description of what had happened in the past few hours. The assistant had started out using quite a few technical terms, such as eighth intercostal and intercostal margins, but reverted to layman's language when she realized she was losing her audience.

The assistant tried to explain the procedure in language everyone could understand. She explained that I had been placed in the supine position, meaning I had been placed on my back. A strap was positioned high up on my chest to allow easy access to the abdominal cavity. A spinal catheter had been inserted to keep spinal fluid pressure within a reasonable range. The catheter was also being used to monitor cerebrospinal pressure. The abdomen, upper thighs and left chest to the clavicle had been prepped and draped. The abdominal cavity had been entered through a midline incision extending from the lower part of the breast bone to the pubis.

Another incision was made starting midway in the first incision and stretching all the way to my side.

All this had been too much information for Raquel. In her mind, she saw blood spurting everywhere. Although she knew that I had been anesthetized, she thought that I was in a great deal of pain, and the thought made her feel faint. She had been standing all the while as the assistant spoke then she sat so abruptly that all attention turned to her. It was obvious that Raquel was on the verge of breaking down. Both her daughters sat down beside her at the same time, acting as prophets, assuring her that their dad was going to be alright as they tried to make her feel better. After ensuring that Raquel was alright, the assistant took her leave, promising the family to keep them informed during the course of the day.

The assistant made a decision, after her briefing session with Raquel and her daughters. She had decided that she would leave the briefing to Dr. Ahmed. She felt that she did not do a good job apprising the family what progress had been made in the operation. Perhaps she had muddied the water and produced the opposite effect to what was intended. That part of the operation she had explained was fairly straightforward in comparison to what was to come. The best thing, therefore, was to leave the briefing in more experienced hands.

Some six hours after the initial briefing, Dr. Ahmed emerged from the Operating Room and headed straight for the Waiting Room. He informed Raquel and the family that the operation was a success. I was in critical, but stable condition, and was in the Open Heart Surgery Recovery Room. There were no mishaps, Dr. Ahmed told them.

The aorta had been repaired; my kidneys were functioning well, and there was no need for concern with respect to my spine. I would be able to walk as soon as I was strong enough to stand. Dr. Ahmed was extremely tired after a grueling nine hours. He would describe the operation and what was accomplished at a later date; in the meantime, he suggested that the family should go home and rest. Dr. Ahmed assured Raquel that she would be advised about any change in my condition.

There was jubilation in the Waiting Room after Raquel, and the family heard the good news. They had to be reminded to keep it down so as not to disturb the other people who were in the Room. The family had gathered up their belongings, left the hospital and headed home. In their euphoria, they had forgotten how cold it was outside, so they did not bundle up as they should have done. They had also forgotten that snow was piled high on the streets and that taxis were hard to find. Those minor inconveniences did not dampen their spirits. If anything they only served to remind them that it was good to be alive and that:

"God was good,
All the time"

14

The Cure

*"Trust in the Lord with all your heart
And lean not on your own understanding
In all your ways acknowledge Him
And He shall direct your paths."
Proverbs 3:5*

Like many others, I knew that passage of Scripture by heart but it did not come to mind during my darkest hours.

I was not sure why I was in that aquarium size tank filled with water with bubbles, from various places, streaming to the top of the tank. Someone kept calling my name, but, try as I might, I could not tell where the voice was coming from or, more importantly, who was calling. But the voice, the call was persistent, almost coaxing me to respond. I would not answer, simply because I did not know who was calling. I remembered my grandmother telling me not to respond to being called unless I knew the caller. According to her, some people prematurely crossed over to the other side because they answered to malevolent spirits.

The voice was not even familiar, just someone calling my name which served to heighten my anxiety. It was most unusual for someone to call me in that manner.

"Anthony!!!"

"Anthony!!!"

The other thing that disturbed me was that no one, except my mother and sister, called me by my given name. I would have recognized the voice if the call had come from either one. In any case, my mother was ruled out immediately because she had been dead for some 15 years and, without a doubt, the voice did not belong to my sister. So I ignored the call, and kept looking around for someone, something to allay my fears.

It seemed to me that fear had become an integral part of my life, my constant companion since I had set foot in Somalia. Before that, I could not remember any time in my life when fear consumed me in that manner. True, I knew what fear was before my Somalia experience. There were some things that engendered fear, like being startled by something that had sent chills up my spine, or being threatened at gunpoint, or being caught in the middle of a fire fight. The fear felt from those experiences were considerably different from the paranoia that had taken over; the paranoia that seemed to have invaded every facet of my life.

There was the fear of treading into the unknown completely vulnerable to whatever it was that could cause me harm. That was the reason why I did not respond to whoever it was that was calling me. If I did not answer then the person, or whatever it was, would leave me alone and I would be able to concentrate on why I was in the tank. Then, I believe, my companion, "Fear", would depart and give me some respite from its damaging effects. I knew that I had been sick and that my body had suffered extensive trauma from disease and medical intervention. Even with those thoughts in mind, it did not occur to me that I must have been sedated, or perhaps that I was hallucinating. I knew that something was not quite right because I had been under water for a considerable length of time, but did not feel the need to surface for air.

At some point, I became aware that I was not alone in the tank. There were other people there, but they all seemed to have been asleep. I was the only one moving around, bumping into others who, like me, were trapped in the tank. The word trapped was ominous. Why did I think I was trapped because, before the word came to mind, I did not have the sense of being imprisoned? I did not feel the need to escape, but now, escape seemed to be my only option.

I remembered being ill and some parts of the operation when bright lights surrounded me and people in blue used their considerable talents to save my life. At that time, I had a sense of being pursued by something malevolent that meant me harm. I remembered having some intuitive feeling that I was required to retrace my foot steps from early childhood to find out why I was not at peace with myself and my life. I could not recall what had happened to my walk down memory lane, and if I had resolved whatever it was that shaped my life. Perhaps I was still groping in the dark and that was why I was in the tank trying desperately to find out what I had left undone?

Although the visibility in the tank was at least 50 feet, I tried to move about looking for a way out without drawing attention to my actions. That seemed necessary, but I could not explain why except that, whoever or whatever was after me, did not know exactly where I was. So I moved stealthily, being directed by my thoughts, to the place that seemed to offer the best means of escape.

But that did not work I could not escape my prison; I could not find a way out. It seemed that the only solution was to respond to the call that had kept on unabated. Notwithstanding that realization,

I hesitated to respond preferring to believe the urban legend that it was in my best interest to know who was calling.

Then as if a light bulb came on, I recognized the voice. It was familiar that's all. Not someone that I knew intimately but that was sufficient and I gravitated towards the sound of the voice. The caller had alternated between Anthony and Mr. Dillett, and it was the tone in the Mr. Dillett that I recognized. It was whispered in my ear. I even felt the breath of the caller on my skin, so I deduced the person was by my side. I opened my eyes, and within my peripheral vision I saw a young man sitting next to me. He was smiling and said in a soft almost coaxing voice:

"You had a really hard time coming out of anesthesia. I could see that you were aware of my presence, but you would not open your eyes. It was as if you were in a coma. You had me worried for a while."

I recognized him as soon as I laid eyes on him. He was one of Dr. Ahmed's assistants who, I assumed, was one of the people in pale blue who had attended to me during my operation. It seemed important to know if he was one of them, but my mouth could not frame the question.

"You are not able to speak," he continued. "So do not even try to respond to me. I just wanted to make sure that you are completely awake and will not slip back into oblivion. Your family is in the Waiting Room anxiously waiting to see you. I will tell them that you are awake, doing well and they should be able to see you in about an hour."

I was totally immobile, not being able to move an inch. Only my eyes could move from one object to the other. I looked at what I saw, and was surprised at the number of tubes protruding from my body. There was the steady beep of monitors to my left and to my right; and next to me was another bed with someone in it. I could not make out the features of the person, only that the bed was occupied with sheets pulled all the way up to the persons chin. That gave me some comfort. The person was alive; if he were dead the sheet would have covered his face also.

Even at that time when it was obvious that there was still a touch and go situation regarding life and death; even as I hovered between the two, I would not pray. It was not as if I did not know better. I knew the consequences of not making my peace with God, but there was an inexplicable obduracy of spirit, turning away from that which would give me life in this world and the next. It was as if I had made a pact with God not to bother Him so long as he did not bother me. Of course, no such pact existed but I acted as if it had been ratified.

I tried to empty my mind of all thoughts except those things that related to my current situation. The pain in my lower abdomen and lower back that I had endured shortly after becoming ill had disappeared. It was replaced with a more intense pain that ran from my chest to my groin. The pain was so intense that my blood pressure spiked and kept rising until a nurse came and administered some medicine to ease the pain. The relief from the pain was instant, and I made a mental note that I would find out what type of medication was so effective. That bit of information seemed to be necessary but I could not figure out why. Perhaps that would come later when I was up and about.

My body may have been totally immobile, but my mind was whirling out of control. So many thoughts, so many things I wanted to know. It seemed important to find out, precisely, what had been done by the people in blue as they utilized their collective expertise, and the expertise of medical professionals outside Lenox Hill circle, to save my life. I wanted to know, at the moment the thought entered my mind, if I had been given a reprieve or if I were on the road to a full recovery.

As I contemplated my situation, I saw my wife approaching me. She was smiling from ear to ear which gave me some comfort. It told me things were going well, and that was precisely what I wanted to know. She did not say anything but still smiling, bent down and kissed me. Without turning, she beckoned over her shoulder and our daughters came into view and were smiling, as effusively, as their mother. No words were uttered, perhaps in deference to me, since I could not speak. But that was not the reason they were speechless. They were speechless because some ten hours earlier; they had expected to see a corpse being wheeled out of the Operating Room. Instead, they were looking at a living, breathing human being.

Without warning, they all started to talk at the same time. My sister and sister-in-law had joined the company by this time. The nurse came and reminded them that they were in the ICU, and they should restrain themselves as best they could. My sister-in-law said that my face was so puffy and battered that I resembled a boxer who had just come through a grueling fight. The description was enough to give me an idea of what I looked like, but whatever or whoever I resembled, I was alive barely or not; I was ***alive.***

Everyone, except my wife was asked to leave after a few minutes. They had caused sufficient disruption in the ICU. It was also apparent that the excitement had been a bit too much for me. I had become tired, and that was easily apparent to my nurse who had been monitoring what was happening around me. I did not know when my wife left as I had fallen asleep. When I awoke all the lights had been dimmed, the room was semi dark, and only the sounds of the monitors broke the silence. I must have fallen asleep again because the next time I woke up most of the lights were on, and I saw Dr. Cahill looking down at me, a smile of satisfaction on his face.

Dr. Cahill spoke at length about the operation, and what had been accomplished. He reiterated again the fact that mine was the most difficult operation that had been attempted by Dr. Ahmed, and indeed that had been done under the auspices of the Hospital. The operation had been successful beyond what they had envisaged. He was ecstatic about the outcome. He said that he did not want to burden me with the details until I was stronger and able to appreciate the hand of God in the process. Having said those things, he left to complete his rounds in the hospital, promising to come back later that day. I wanted him to stay to absorb more of his energy, and the comfort I felt in his presence.

Like a new born babe, I slept most of the time. Unlike a baby, however, I had to be fed intravenously. There were tubes in my bladder and stomach to take away the waste and tubes to drain the incisions. But those things were of little importance as I thought about my situation lying helpless in a hospital bed, waiting for my wife and daughters to come and sit with me for short periods. The visits broke the monotony of just lying there. I could listen to their chatter even if I could not respond. Their voices were like music to my ears.

Dr. Ahmed came to see me late in the day following my operation. Actually he had visited several times before but I was not aware of his presence. He had checked the charts, examined me thoroughly and had given specific instructions to the nurse on my care. No chances were to be taken. Dr. Ahmed just stood there looking at me before undertaking his examination. He was pleased with my progress, so far, and said as much. He did not expect me to answer but observed me with expert eyes. No doubt he would have detected any change in my countenance, and would have addressed that if I seemed puzzled or agitated. I must have been satisfied by what he had to say because he went through the process of briefing me, and after about fifteen minutes he left.

I might have been immobile, but my brain worked overtime assessing the character and expertise of my nurses and Dr. Ahmed's assistants who made their rounds at all times of day and night. My wife was also in tune with my feelings. Perhaps her constant vigilance in keeping tabs on me, since I became ill, had honed her ability to read my mind. An incident occurred that gave me the peace of mind that I was safe, not only in terms of the medical expertise of my doctors, but because I had an advocate to ensure my well-being.

My first nurse in the Open Heart Surgery ICU was efficient and compassionate. She also had a heavy Irish brogue as if she had just stepped off the boat. She exuded an air of competence mingled with tenderness that was reassuring. I felt at ease with her. Although there was no verbal communication, she knew how I felt from the look in my eyes. My wife also liked her and seemed to relinquish some of her vigilance when that nurse was on duty. Sadly, I do not remember her name but she, nonetheless, remained in my thoughts as an example of a dedicated nurse. The nurses worked 12-hour shifts, and I was satisfied with all of them, except one.

She came on duty at 2000 hours one night. I became agitated no sooner she had taken over. I had a sense that something would go wrong. Since I was powerless to help myself, my anxiety manifested itself in an increase in my heart rate and my blood pressure spiked. I could not control my emotions, no matter how hard I tried. My blood pressure continued to rise. The nurse tried to calm me down, but her efforts exacerbated my anxiety. The nurse thought that my operation had to do with my discomfort and contacted Dr. Ahmed to report on my condition. Dr. Ahmed then called Raquel and suggested that she should go to the hospital immediately. He did not think what was going on was life threatening, but felt her presence in the ICU was essential.

Raquel had only arrived home about fifteen minutes before she received Dr. Ahmed's call. Needless to say she panicked although she was told that I was not in danger. She left home in a hurry with Jenni and Melanie, relaying what Dr. Ahmed had told her. They caught a taxi at the corner of 90 Street and Columbus Avenue and actually told the driver to step on the gas. The taxi sped down Columbus, turned left on 86th Street and went through Central Park. The first light they encountered was at the corner of 86th and Fifth Avenue. The driver made an illegal turn on Fifth Avenue before the light had changed to green.

They were not inconvenienced by anymore red lights, so their next stop was in front of the Hospital. Raquel thanked the driver for his understanding, paid the fare with a generous tip, got out of the taxi and went directly to the ICU. At that late hour, after visiting hours, Raquel would have had to register at the Security Desk. However, the guard knew her, so he just waved her and the girls through.

Dr. Ahmed was there when they arrived. He had my blood pressure under control, and my heart rate was back to normal. Dr. Ahmed had taken the nurse out of earshot and questioned her about what had happened to have given me a panic attack. She did not have a clue about what had thrown me into that state. While Dr. Ahmed spoke to the nurse, Raquel came and sat next to my bed. She held my hand and asked me what was wrong even though she knew I could not respond verbally. However, my eyes told the story. She told me later on that my eyes kept darting from her face to the nurse. Raquel was so attuned to my feelings she deduced immediately that, for whatever reason, I did not feel safe with the nurse. Raquel relayed her thoughts to Dr. Ahmed, and within half an hour another nurse was in attendance.

After a week in the ICU, I was transferred to a step down ICU and a few days later I was placed in a regular hospital room. As I gained strength in the days that followed, the tubes were removed, including the catheters. Intravenous feeding was replaced with foods, such as mashed potatoes with gravy, noodles and Ensure. I had so much "Ensure" that it took several years after leaving the hospital before I could even taste the drink. I was also made to do light exercises and was forced by nurses or my wife to walk the corridors of the hospital. More often than not, I complained about being weak and tired, but my protests were generally met with "we understand." No one indulged me, particularly not my wife.

My body functions had returned to normal, and after three weeks in the hospital, I was being prepared to go home. However, I was slowly sinking into a depression that eventually took hold of me, and at one point, threatened to derail my recovery. I thought I needed to see a psychiatrist, not so much so because I wanted someone to get into my head. I felt that seeing a psychiatrist would have been the quickest way for me to get medication to make me feel better. Dr. Cahill did not think that my problem was in my head, but rather was physically induced because I had only recently undergone an extensive and invasive operation.

Dr. Cahill came to see me every day and spent time talking to both me and Raquel, trying to get us to see that medical intervention was not the answer. He was concerned that I could become addicted to whatever drug might be prescribed. It was much better, he said, for me to come to terms with my feelings without drugs. But, as the day drew nearer for my discharge from the hospital, the panic, that was mild at first increased in intensity.

There were other stressful situations that caused me to panic whenever I thought about them or when I was forced to be cognizant of what was to come. One of the resultant effects of the repair to my aorta was, according Dr. Ahmed, a lifelong dependence on antibiotics. Every care was going to be taken to make sure that I was bacteria free otherwise the aortic graft could be compromised. The fact immunologists were against using antibiotics over long periods, was not taken into consideration at that time. Compromising the health of my aorta was not an option, so I had to take antibiotics.

It was for that reason I was taught, while I was in the hospital, to keep up with a regiment of antibiotics that was to be administered intravenously. To that end, a catheter was placed in my subclavian artery. Detailed instructions were given on how to maintain the catheter to avoid infections. Thinking about what could happen if I became infected was sufficient to send me into a depression.

The dangers of losing my kidneys had receded into the distant past as was the possibility of paralysis from mistakes that might have been made during the operation. The most troubling aspect of my illness and recovery was the possibility that the graft might rupture, and could do so without any warning. The indication that the graft was not holding would manifest itself in excruciating pain just below the left rib cage. In that eventuality the prognosis was that I would die from excessive bleeding, even if I were in the hospital. That probability was like a death sentence that caused me to panic every time I felt, or thought I felt, a pain below my rib cage. I was glad to be alive, of course, but the stress of what could happen was not conducive to a speedy recovery.

I thought about how fortunate I was, to have a dedicated wife, family and friends. I had regular visits from friends and colleagues from UNDP. During one of those visits someone from Human Resources told me that, when I was well enough to return to work, I should consider an assignment to the UNDP office in Copenhagen, Denmark. No more hardship duty stations for me, he had said;

instead I would be able to enjoy a normal existence, with my family, in one of the most coveted spots in the world.

The rest of my stay in the hospital was uneventful, and my health continued to improve. There was some concern that I would have been unable to climb the twelve stairs to our apartment. However, those fears were put to rest when I managed to navigate six steps in the Rehab Center with ease.

The day I left the hospital was cold and uninviting. The sun had decided to take the day off, and the clouds hung low in the sky, threatening another round of snow that would paralyze the city even further. Cars parked on the streets were hidden from view by snow that the snow removal crews had pushed aside to clear the streets. The ride home was most uncomfortable. My inside jiggled each time the taxi hit potholes that were too numerous to count, if I were so inclined. I had no difficulties climbing the stairs to our apartment, but was zapped of what little strength I had. My wife made me comfortable in a recliner she had bought, specifically for the anticipated long recovery that lay ahead.

She sat in a sofa next to the recliner and, for the first time since the ordeal began, we cried together. They were soothing tears, cleansing tears as if we were attempting to wash away the months of anxiety and stress. They were also tears of relief. She did not have to be afraid anymore each time she passed a Funeral Home. Such a place that attended to the dead could not pull me into its vortex; into a place of no return. She did not have to worry about those unwelcome thoughts anymore but they came, uninvited to her mind. The road ahead was still fraught with many unknown variables but we were home, together. We cried recounting the difficult times when it seemed that my life was over; we also recalled the triumphant times when the light shone through and I was on the road to recovery.

I do not remember how long we sat there just holding hands and basking in our new found peace. It must have been a long time because, by the time we became aware of our surroundings, the street lamps, seen through the panoramic window of our apartment, were lit. Darkness had already descended on the city without our being aware of it. We did not have anywhere to go, so we sat mostly in silence, savoring each other's company.

By the time I was released from the hospital, Melanie had returned to Spelman College in Atlanta and Jenni had resumed her studies at New York University. Alex, after trying unsuccessfully to enter the US, was back in Belize. Raquel and I spoke about the proposed assignment to Denmark and decided that was not the place for us at that time. Winter in New York was tolerable, cold with overcast skies, some days, but bearable. On the other hand winter in Denmark was cold, bleak, damp and above all, the sun was usually missing in action for about four months during the year. We were not prepared to face seasonal affective disorder or SAD, so I turned down the assignment and opted for an appointment as Classification Officer in Human Resources in New York instead.

A few days after leaving the hospital, I was admitted once more to repair the sutures in my abdomen. I had unwittingly torn some stitches when I tried to arrest lying down too quickly. I was sitting with my legs stretched out on the sofa. I decided to lie down and was in the process of doing so when I realized that I was descending too fast and that my head would hit the arm of the sofa. I tried to slow the rate of descent by grabbing the back of the sofa. I felt a searing pain that persisted for more than half an hour, so I called Dr. Ahmed and told him what had happened. The next day I was in his office at which time he scheduled the operation to repair the broken sutures.

I had two other operations over the course of the following year. The first was to insert a mesh to assist in strengthening my stomach muscles. The mesh did not hold; therefore, it had to be replaced. It broke again, but I refused to have another operation with the result that I look like someone who has imbibed too many beers. It became necessary for me to wear a binder since the weight of my protruding stomach placed a strain on my back. Over the years I also developed stenosis of the spine that is extremely painful. Walking for long distance became next to impossible and hiking in hilly areas stretched my tolerance for pain to its limits.

We settled into a fairly enjoyable routine of living in New York City. Broadway and its allure were some fifty blocks from our apartment. We could walk to museums, Lincoln Center and Carnegie Hall, if we were so inclined; or we could take a bus if walking was out of the question. I was also on a mission to sample most, if not all, the cuisines that were available in the multi-cultural City. Chinese, Italian, Indian, Pakistani, Greek and Caribbean foods were enticing additions to my wife's excellent cooking skills. Within a few months after leaving the hospital, I had gained back the forty pounds I lost during my illness. I had also stopped smoking. My metabolism changed so unwanted pounds crept up on me. One day, at a routine medical examination, I tipped the scale at 190 pounds, the most I had ever weighed in my entire life.

I returned to work in September 1993, still not fully recovered, but a few hours in the office were better than being at home twiddling my thumbs. I also wanted to get away, at least for a short time, from my wife's constant reminder of my miraculous healing. Actually, I think that it was my conscience that was getting the better of me, because, in reality, my wife seldom mentioned the "miracle". She did not mention it, but I saw her disappointment in my "not getting it" every time her gaze remained on me for too long. On reflection, I think she was, in fact, marveling at how far I had come and that she was relieved of the tremendous burden of constantly making sure I was doing well.

15

Revelation

*"Here's the amazing thing —
light trumps darkness, every time.
You can stick a light into the dark,
but you can't stick the dark into the light"*
(Unknown)

For some unfathomable reason, I did not see my wife's inner peace and obvious relief that the long night was behind us, and that our future looked bright once more. I thought I was being forced into believing what she and Dr. Cahill believed. I felt pressured to accept, as true, that prayers and petitions to the Almighty had everything to do with my getting well. I was not sure why I was so obdurate in refusing to acknowledge the hand of God in my reprieve from death. I was neither an agnostic nor an atheist. In actual fact, I was born a Methodist. What that meant was that I was baptized in the Methodist Church, went to Sunday school and attended a Methodist Primary School.

In my early teenage years, I went to hear a fiery preacher who was conducting a crusade just around the corner from where I lived. He scared the living lights out of me with his hell and damnation sermons. He conjured up images of what eternity was going to be in a place called Hades where the unrighteous burned forever and ever. There was the visual image, graphically portrayed in words, about the rich man who ended up hell, and could not get anyone to place a drop of water on his tongue to quench his thirst.

I was sure the preacher also spoke about Christ dying on the cross for my sins, and what He went through before succumbing to death to redeem those who accepted Him. That is the center of the Christian belief system, but what became the driving force in my conversion was what would happen to me in the end if I did not accept Christ, and be born again.

One night after listening to a sermon that portrayed a more damning future for the unsaved, I decided to give my life to the Lord. About a month later I was baptized, became a part of the congregation that had sponsored the crusade, and tried to live up to what was expected in the Evangelical community. But the reason for the change in my life was not centered on what Christ had done for me; but rather on what I should do to escape the torments of hell for an eternity. Fear kept me going through the motions, but eventually that fear gave way to nonchalance. Then the lure of the forbidden pleasures of the flesh took over. Added to my problem was the absence of a moral compass I did not possess. If I had, it would have guided me through those difficult years.

So I went astray and before long I was indulging in the transient pleasures of the flesh. I drifted so far that, at one point in my life, I convinced myself that I was safe and that I would have enough time to repent in the event death came calling. But I did not reckon with the dwindling warmth of fellowship with professing Christians. I stayed away, and soon the Apostle Paul's injunction about not forsaking the fellowship of Christians was forgotten like so many other things.

I had heard a story about a man named Tom. He had given his life to Christ and went to Church regularly, not only on Sundays, but also during the week for prayer meetings and Bible studies. He even became a deacon, but, for whatever reason, he drifted away. Eventually, he stopped going to Church, avoided his Christian brothers and sisters and even stopped answering their phone calls. One day the Pastor went uninvited, to Tom's home. The day was cold, so cold that it made your cheeks numb if you stayed outside too long. The Pastor and Tom sat in front of the fireplace absorbing the welcomed heat, not saying a word to each other at first.

The Pastor opened the dialogue by asking Tom about his health, his work and how the weather was treating him. Not a word was said about why Tom had stopped going to Church. After a while, the Pastor got up, took a thong and removed a red hot piece of coal from the fire. He sat down again, and they continued their conversation. Pretty soon the piece of coal lost its heat. The red glow disappeared and was replaced by a dull gray hue that soon became cold to the touch. The Pastor then said goodbye and left. The symbolism of the piece of coal turning cold when taken from the fire was not lost on Tom. About a week after the Pastor visited him, Tom was back at Church, and before long he had resumed his activities there.

I guessed I must have lost my way as Tom had done. The difference between us was that I did not have someone like Tom's Pastor in my life. So I drifted and the warmth of fellowship, and everything associated with living a Christian life deserted me. Or rather, I deserted that way of life. I might have lost my way, but someone was looking out for me. Someone was praying that I would find my way back to the Lord.

My wife did not sit idly by waiting for me to come to my senses. She knew what path she was going to take to renew her life long quest for spiritual enlightenment. She had been a Church goer from her youth but, like me, had drifted from the path. We did not go to

Church as a family. As a matter of fact, there were no dedication or baptism services for our girls. We prayed at every meal, and we read Bible stories to them as children. We even prayed with them before they went to bed at nights until they were able to pray by themselves. So God, and the Christian faith were not altogether alien to us.

My wife had, in fact, gone to Church sporadically when we were assigned to Sierra Leone in 1985. Her church attendance became more frequent when we went to Zimbabwe in 1988. By that time Jenni was in boarding school in London. Melanie went to church with her mother quite often but I only went with them on occasions. I went but my heart was not in it, I did so to please my wife. Melanie became very involved in the Church, and was baptized in Harare a few months before we were reassigned to New York in 1991. The spiritual aspect of my wife's life was not totally void. There was a spark there that was ignited by Dr. Cahill when he confessed that only God could have saved my life. But before that time God was not an integral part of our lives.

Later on when we had turned our lives around, a friend said to Jenni that she and the family must have been regular Church folks when she and her sister were growing up. Her response was a succinct:

"No, we went to the beach."

That was pretty much how we spent most of our Sundays. We joined friends for picnics on the beach in places like Angola, Antigua, Jamaica and Sierra Leone where there were fantastic beaches.

The past was the past, and my wife decided that she would order her life to include worshiping God, with other Christians, even if it meant leaving me behind. That was not her choice, to leave me in my unbelief if that was what I wanted. But she knew what she had to do to follow the desires of her heart.

Unlike when we were abroad I tagged along to please my wife when she went to Church. We went to several Churches in New York City and Brooklyn trying to find a place where she was comfortable. Times Square Church and Brooklyn Tabernacle were, she believed, God inspired churches with Scripture based teaching and fantastic choirs. Both were mega churches, too big for my wife's taste so we kept looking for a congregation that would satisfy her spiritual needs. She was becoming anxious and I could feel her angst at the time it was taking to find a church that was suitable for her.

One Saturday night, in the winter of 1996, we were trying to make up our minds which Church we were going to visit the following day. Out of the blue I said to my wife:

"Let's go to that church you had visited when I was in Somalia."

Her reply came immediately:

"Isn't that something, I was thinking about the same place just a few minutes ago?"

The next day, Sunday, we went to Central Baptist Church that had been revealed to us, about the same time, the night before. It was located on Manhattan's Upper West Side. At first I was sorry that we did not go to one of the other Churches, mostly because the atmosphere in the Church was drab and uninviting. That day, the temperature outside the Church was about 35 degree F, and a few degrees lower inside. The praise team left a lot to be desired, and the sermon was not uplifting. There were only about 50 people in attendance, most of whom were aloof. However, there were two people at that service who made impressions on us.

One was a middle aged lady named Mary. She was warm and outgoing and made us feel like longtime friends. We promised her that we would be back and genuinely planned to do so. The other person was a rotund, elderly gentleman, an Assistant Pastor named Jacobs, Pastor Ron Jacobs. There was something endearing about him. His shirt under his ill-fitting jacket was rumpled, and the cuffs were frayed, but his personality drew us to him. We were back at the Church the next week and the weeks, months and years that followed until we started to attend another Church in Queens, New York.

Pastor Jacobs had a history of his own, and perhaps that was what made each conversation with him so interesting. He was from a prominent Jewish mafia family and had converted to Christianity when, according to him, he was a guest of the Federal government in Atlanta, Georgia. One day my wife asked him how it was that he was allowed to leave the organization. He said that he had to give a solemn oath that he would not divulge or speak about anything to do with his previous associations. If he kept his word, he had said, then he and his family would be safe otherwise… He did not finish the sentence but left it to our imagination to deduce what would have happen to them.

In addition to having a captivating personality, Pastor Jacobs was an excellent teacher who made characters like Moses, Daniel, David, Paul and yes Jesus come to life. He also taught about the Tribulation, about angels and how the Cherubim scared him out of his wits.

About two months after we started to attend the Church on a regular basis, we became Pastor Jacob's students in a Sunday school class. And that was the start of my way back trying to find what I had misplaced in my youth. Most Christians I know can recall the exact date, sometimes even the hour, when they turned their lives around. Not so with me. My conversion was gradual, over a period of time that I cannot define. As a matter of fact, I am not even able to say when the realization, that I had turned my life around, hit me. Suffice it to say, I woke up one morning feeling a little more at peace than the mornings before.

Then one day, as I read a passage of Scripture relating to my Sunday school class, I felt a calm wash over me that I did not remember feeling before. It was somewhat similar to being in the dark for a long time and then, voila, the lights came on. There was still some level of skepticism in the power of God's redemptive grace. There was still some fear of the unknown that I could not identify, but the cynicism and dread I had felt before seemed to be receding. I did not try to analyze the feeling. All I knew was that I felt as if I was in a better place without the benefit of consciously making a comparison with how I felt before.

We had been studying Revelation Chapter 3 in our Sunday school class. I was particularly intrigued with what was said to the Church at Sardis. I was fascinated with the command in verse 2 in which the Church was told to wake up and strengthen what was about to die. I wondered if that were a reference to what was happening to me, or what was going to happen if I did not wake up. But the verse that really took hold, and became one of my favorite passages of Scripture was verse 20.

"Behold I stand at the door and knock. If anyone hears My voice and opens the door, I will come in to him and dine with him, and he with me."

Perhaps that was the beginning of lifting the veil of doubt and disbelief from my soul. It was like building blocks, where one premise is added on the other and somewhere down the line the whole picture comes into sharp relief. Up to that point nothing was crystal clear. Things were clearer than they were before, but I was still not there yet. However, I no longer had an option to view the Church from afar. I had to become involved. It was important to me to know how it worked, and how people functioned in a living breathing Christian community.

In addition to the classes with Pastor Jacobs, I took a course of study entitled "Abundant Life". The teacher for that class, Chris Phillips, became a friend over the years that followed and a spiritual guide during very difficult times. I do not recall who my class mates were, but I remember that I grew spiritually, strengthened by the power of the Gospel. I understood, for the first time the depth of what Christ suffered to redeem *me* from certain damnation.

My wife and I also spent a considerable time in Bible studies and, before long, we had committed to a three year program of study in practical theology, a ministry of Mission to the Americas entitled URBACAD short for Urban Academy. We attended weekly seminars delving into doctrine, New Testament history and geography. We studied eschatology, hermeneutics and the life of Christ through the prisms of Mathew and other writers. We completed projects on different subjects. For example, I was fascinated with the study of cults and read several books on the subject including "Kingdom of the Cults" by Walter Martin. I even taught a course on the topic of cults during my second year of URBACAD studies.

I had come a long way from those days when I would not acknowledge that there was a significant difference in my life when the faith and prayers of believers had brought me through. I might not have been totally conscious of the gravity of my situation. That, no doubt, was the reason for my nonchalance even in the face of overwhelming odds of my surviving the disease that had ravaged my body. But others believed and prayed and like the friends of the paralytic man in the Bible, who found a way to get him to Jesus' side, their faith was sufficient for the miracle that ensued.

"When Jesus saw their faith he said "Friend, your sins are forgiven". Luke 5:20

I was the beneficiary of that kind of faith, and was grateful that I had family and friends who prayed for me, and had faith to believe that God would, and did answer their prayers. However, even as I was making my way into the light and my faith grew with each passing day, I was still plagued with the fear of death. I kept wondering what it would be like when my time came. There were times when I thought about those last moments and fear gripped me since I had not, up to that point in my life, given myself over completely to the will of God.

As a result of my uncertainty about what awaited me on the other side, Dr. Ahmed's prophesy kept me awake at nights, and fear took over at the slightest hint of pain just below my right rib cage.

Epilogue

The Man at the Gate

"If you are distressed by anything external, the pain is not due to the thing itself but to your own estimate of it; and this you have the power to revoke at any moment."
Marcus Aurelius

The pain, just below my rib cage, left just as suddenly as it had manifested itself. In its wake was a dull ache that indicated I was still alive, and had not been transported to another place. It seemed as if I had been lying in my bed in the fetal position for hours going over what had happened in Somalia and the events that followed. In reality the hour hand of the clock, on the night stand, had only moved half way between two and three o'clock.

At one point as the pain reached a crescendo, I heard something assuring me with the words, "I have your back". The assurance came from my innermost self, not from a voice that spoke, but rather from my subconscious telling me not to panic, that all would be well in time. I remembered making a conscious decision that the episodes of debilitating pain would not, in the future, send me into a panic. I had said, not with my voice but with the same medium that had assured me all would be well, that I was in God's hands. I would not allow any condition, whatever it was, to rob me of the assurance that all would be well, whether I lived or died.

I did not know why I had panicked and why I had been overcome with such an overwhelming fear of dying. I had not felt such fear even at the height of my illness. Then, when I had made my peace with God, death held such terror that touched me at the deepest level of my soul.

The pain was no longer evident; it had dissipated as had the fear of dying. I had been scared out of my wits, believing that Dr. Ahmed's predictions were in fact coming true. I was so centered on the possibility of the graft rupturing that I had forgotten other aspects of my recovery and the healing process. I had forgotten that Dr. Ahmed had also warned about possible side effects of the Splenectomy that could be present as in the missing limb syndrome. The pain I felt had nothing to do with the graft, but rather my body searching for the missing spleen.

Regardless of the reason or reasons for my failing body to act up, and I was certain that many instances would be manifested in the future, I had decided to place my hand in the hand of God as the poet, Marie Louise Haskins, said so many years ago:

"And I said to the man who stood at the gate of the year:
Give me a light that I may tread safely into the unknown!

And he replied:
Go out into the darkness and put your hand into the Hand of God. That shall be to you better than light and safer than a known way.

So, I went forth, and finding the Hand of God, trod gladly into the night…"

About the Author

Anthony Dillett retired from the United Nations Development Programme (UNDP) in 1996 after 25 years of service. During that time he acquired excellent skills in Project Management and General and Personnel Administration. He was assigned to Somalia in 1992 as Operations Manager (OM) where, in addition to the regular duties of OM, he oversaw the re-establishment of the Somalia Office after some five years of civil war. He was also instrumental in launching a support office in Nairobi, Kenya with the outbreak of renewed hostilities in mid-1993. Since leaving the UNDP in 1996, Mr. Dillett served as a consultant for Blue Print Management Group Inc., and as Project Manager with the Kutwal Group. He Lives in Atlanta, Georgia with his wife, Raquel. He has four children, seven grandchildren and one great grandchild.

Made in the USA
Charleston, SC
28 March 2015